RULES FOR
SPIRITUAL
INITIATION

RULES FOR SPIRITUAL INITIATION

ZACHARY F. LANSDOWNE

SAMUEL WEISER, INC.
York Beach, Maine

First published in 1990 by
Samuel Weiser, Inc.
Box 612
York Beach, Maine 03910

Library of Congress Cataloging-In-Publication Data

Lansdowne, Zachary F.
    Rules for spiritual initiation / Zachary Lansdowne.

    Includes bibliographical references.
    1. Theosophy.   2. Spiritual life.   I. Title.
    BP565.L214R85   1990
    299'.934--dc20   90-38635
    ISBN 0-87728-707-4   CIP

Cover illustration ©Michael Martin, 1990

Typeset in 11 point Baskerville
Printed in the United States of America by
Baker Johnson, Inc.

Contents

List of Tables

Acknowledgments

Appreciation is expressed to the following individuals for their careful and thoughtful comments on an earlier version of this book: Elizabeth Douphner, Pamela Moore, and Brigitte Terseur. Appreciation is also expressed to the Lucis Publishing Company for permission to quote from the several books by Alice A. Bailey.

Introduction

In 1922, Alice A. Bailey published fourteen symbolic rules for spiritual initiation, with only a very limited and fragmentary explanation. The purpose of this book is to clarify those rules and give a complete explanation, showing that each rule has both an outer and an inner meaning. The outer interpretation embodies a character-building or purificatory objective that has been proclaimed by all of the great religions down through the centuries; the inner interpretation embodies an injunction on meditation that the aspirant for initiation needs to study and obey. Thus, each rule gives instruction for the two phases in every aspirant's life: the outer life of practice and the inner life of concentration, or the outer ability to express holy living and the inner ability to contact the higher self.

It may be helpful to distinguish between *laws*, *commands*, and *rules*. The laws of nature, such as the law of gravity or the laws of thermodynamics, govern and control everything that happens in time and space. These laws cannot be avoided or denied; if they are broken, infringed, or evaded, they carry their own penalty within themselves. Commands are orders issued by people in authority, who believe they are in a position to dominate and enforce their orders. For instance, the obligations to pay taxes and report for military duty are commands that are often avoided and ignored. Rules are the result of age-long experience and do not assume the form of either laws or commands. When recognized by those for whom they exist, rules evoke a prompt, intuitive response. They need no enforcement but are voluntarily accepted, with the belief that they provide the conditions needed for success. This book examines a set of rules that provide instruction for progressing on the spiritual path.

In theosophy, the spiritual path is divided into several distinct segments. The first segment is called the *path of probation*. Every aspirant starts to travel on this segment after acknowledging that an inner conflict exists between the personality (or lower self) and the soul (or higher self). The Apostle Paul referred to this conflict when he wrote: "For what I would, that do I not; but what I hate, that do I" (Rom. 7:15). Because of this inner conflict, the aspirant begins to see the need for disciplining the personality and invoking the intuitive voice of the soul for guidance. The path of probation ends with an expansion of consciousness that is called the first spiritual initiation. The second segment is called the *path of discipleship*; it commences with the first initiation, continues through the second initiation, and ends with the third initiation. The third segment is called the *path of initiation*; it starts with the third initiation and continues through still higher initiations.

Let us consider the meaning of these ideas in more detail. The word *initiation* signifies entrance into something. *Spiritual initiation* refers to entrance into the spiritual life, or into a fresh stage in that life, and can be characterized as an expansion of consciousness during which one becomes aware that a certain range of subjective knowledge is one's own. It refers to a moment in which the spiritual self within the personality becomes aware of being the soul, with soul powers, soul relationships, and soul purpose. And it is a step out of the human kingdom of nature into a superhuman one.

The concept of dividing the spiritual path into distinct stages can be found outside theosophy. For instance, it is possible to relate each spiritual initiation to a specific stage of development in Christian mysticism, Hinduism, Buddhism, and yoga. Also, the mysteries of spiritual initiation can be found within the symbolic numbers, rituals, and words of Masonic ceremonies. When correctly presented and rightly interpreted, those ceremonies provide the teaching needed to pass from darkness to Light, from the unreal to the Real, and from death to Immortality. However, Masonic ceremonies are difficult to interpret because they are based on a structure of Hebrew names and nomenclature that are thousands of years old and long out of date.

What is the significance of the rules for spiritual initiation discussed here? These rules, when rightly interpreted, provide a concrete statement of the intuitive guidance that is progressively received on the spiritual path. If we are not yet ready for a particular rule, then we can receive from it only a hint of the technique to which we will later be exposed. If we are ready for the rule, which means that we recognize it as an injunction needing to be obeyed, then we can voluntarily apply it to our lives. Or if we have already passed beyond a particular rule, we may simply remark: "This I have known."

There are fourteen rules, forming two different sequences of seven rules. According to our interpretation, the first sequence provides elementary instructions for the path of probation, and the second sequence provides advanced instructions for the path of discipleship.[1] These two sequences can be thought of as having a linear relationship: After we master the elementary rules, we are guided to begin the advanced rules. Because each rule in the second sequence provides a higher meaning of the corresponding rule in the first sequence, these two sequences show that the spiritual path forms a spiral rather than a straight line. Spiritual development can be likened to climbing a mountain, and the spiritual path to a spiral formed around the outside of the mountain.

Because each rule is written in a symbolic way, it can be interpreted as providing two different injunctions: one describing a character-building or purificatory objective and one describing a stage in the process of meditation. Thus, these rules actually yield four different sequences of training. Based on the first seven rules, chapter 1 provides elementary instructions for character building, and chapter 2 provides elementary instructions for meditation. Based on the last seven rules, chapter 3 provides advanced instructions for character building, and chapter 4 provides advanced instructions for meditation.

In theosophy, a *ray* is defined as a particular quality of energy, and altogether, seven different rays are described. In recent years, there has been considerable interest in the seven rays, and a number of authors have investigated the relationships existing between the rays and such topics as philosophy, psychology, yoga, healing, and even foreign affairs. In each sevenfold sequence of instruction for the paths of probation and discipleship, as well as for character building and meditation, each rule carries the specific quality associated with the corresponding ray, as shown in chapter 5.

Consequently, Bailey's rules for spiritual initiation are extraordinary: They provide concrete formulations of the intuitive guidance that is progressively received on the spiritual path, characterizations of the spiral nature of that guidance, the similarities and differences between the paths of probation and discipleship, the interrelationship between character building and meditation, and the connection between the process of initiation and the seven rays.

Bailey published these rules in the first of a series of about twenty books that she wrote over a thirty-year period. The rules actually anticipated her entire canon of teaching because the clues needed for understanding them are scattered throughout all of her books. In the chapters that follow, comprehensive sets of notes identify where the various aspects of each rule are discussed in those books.

Chapter 1

Elementary Rules for Character Building

To understand the nature of the spiritual path, it is helpful to review some concepts from theosophy. Every human being consists of a personality, a soul, and a spirit. The *personality* has four aspects: The mental body or mind gives the power of discrimination; the emotional body gives the capacity to sense, desire, aspire, and attract; the vital or etheric body gives the power to act and be energetic; and the dense physical body, which is controlled by the three preceding aspects, enables activity to take place in the physical world. The *soul* has three primary aspects: will or purpose, inclusive love, and wisdom. The informing, indwelling soul seeks to impress, impel, and motivate the personality. The personality and the soul are in turn animated and impelled by the *spirit*, which is the energy of life itself.

The spiritual path is divided into several distinct segments, corresponding to the various initiations, and each segment has a definite curriculum. The word *aspirant* connotes someone on the path of probation, which extends from the beginning of the spiritual path to the first initiation. The main lesson of each aspirant is learning to express the love aspect of the soul through outer behavior. A *disciple* is someone on the path of discipleship, which extends from the first to the third initiations. The main lesson of each disciple is learning to express the various aspects of the soul through the mental, emotional, and etheric bodies, resulting in what is called the soul-infused personality. An *initiate* refers to someone on the path of initiation, which extends from the third to still higher initiations. The main lesson of each initiate is learning to integrate the soul-infused personality with the spirit.

The path of probation is divided into two distinct stages, called Little Chelaship and Chela in the Light. *Chela* is a Sanskrit word meaning spiritual servant or disciple. During the first stage, or Little Chelaship, aspirants seek out and are instructed by various teachers in the physical world. During the second stage, or Chela in the Light, they slowly learn to be guided by the light of their own souls, which explains that particular name.

Character building is defined as the effort to express the soul attitude, soul awareness, and soul consciousness, through the medium of the personality, in the physical world. In this chapter, the first seven of Bailey's rules for initiation are interpreted as describing a sevenfold process of character building for the path of probation. Rules One through Three give instruction for the first stage of that path, Little Chelaship; and rules Four through Seven give instruction for the second stage, Chela in the Light.

Bailey scattered a mass of information about initiation through all of her books, written over many years. In her final book, she stated that this information needs to be collated and brought together as a basis for instructing individuals in training for initiation.[1] The purpose of the present book is to interpret her rules for initiation by collating and bringing together her many scattered fragments. Although based on Bailey's own material, these interpretations are solely the responsibility of the present writer and may not be what was originally intended. Thus, the reader must carefully judge the accuracy of the interpretations that follow.

Rule One

> Let the disciple search within the heart's deep cave. If there the fire burns bright, warming his brother yet heating not himself, the hour has come for making application to stand before the door.[2]

Before interpreting this rule, it is necessary to review some additional concepts. According to theosophy, the solar system is divided into seven force fields, called *planes*. Only three planes are discussed in this book: the physical; the emotional, or astral; and the mental. Each of these planes is further divided into seven subplanes. In the case of the physical plane, the names of the seven subplanes are first ether, second ether, third ether, fourth ether, gaseous, liquid, and solid. The three lowest physical subplanes—gaseous, liquid, and solid—compose the dense world of matter and are perceptible with the five physical senses. The four highest physical subplanes represent the etheric region. Although imperceptible with normal faculties, these four ethers are considered part of the physical realm.

Corresponding to the division of the physical plane into dense and etheric portions, a person's physical body also has two portions. The *dense physical body* is composed of solids, liquids, and gases, including such parts as the bones, blood system, nervous system, brain, and endocrine glands. The *etheric body*, sometimes called the vital body, is composed of the four ethers. Although of a tenuous nature, the etheric body is the framework or foundation underlying every part of the dense physical body, and it vitalizes or energizes the dense physical cells.

Table 1. The Major Etheric Chakras

English Name	Sanskrit Name	Approximate Location	Endocrine Gland
Crown	Sahasrara	Top of head	Pineal
Brow	Ajna	Between the eyebrows, in front of head	Pituitary
Throat	Vishuddha	Back of neck	Thyroid
Heart	Anahata	Between shoulder blades	Thymus
Solar plexus	Manipura	Well below shoulder blades	Pancreas
Sacral	Svadhisthana	Lower part of lumbar area	Gonads
Basic	Muladhara	Base of spine	Adrenals

Source: A. A. Bailey, *The Soul and Its Mechanism* (1930; reprint; New York: Lucis Publishing Company, 1976), 111, 120.

The word *chakra* means "wheel" in Sanskrit; it refers to a subtle wheel of energy, or force center, in the etheric body. Traditional yoga philosophy recognizes the existence of seven major etheric chakras. For each of these chakras, Table 1 lists the English name, traditional Sanskrit name, approximate location, and associated endocrine gland. The rest of this book refers to the chakras by their English names.

The first rule describes the beginning of the path of probation as well as the overall objective for that path. In this rule, the symbols have the following interpretations: "The heart's deep cave" refers to the heart chakra; "fire burns bright," to compassion, which is the quality associated with the heart chakra; "brother," to another human being; "making application," to practicing self-discipline and purification; and "door," to the first initiation.

Each phrase of this rule is interpreted separately. The first phrase is "let the disciple search within the heart's deep cave." Because of their ambition to achieve material success, individuals who are approaching the spiritual path have already attained enough alignment with the soul to utilize their faculty of abstract thought, representing the wisdom aspect of the soul. Because of this alignment, they also have gained the potential of sensing feelings of oneness with others, such as sympathy and compassion. These feelings are sensed within the heart chakra and represent the love aspect of the soul. Since awareness of these feelings leads to inner conflict, people initially wish to suppress or ignore them. Although such suppression does bring temporary relief to the personality, it also arrests and delays the work of the soul. The meaning of the first phrase of the first rule is that people should not try to suppress or ignore their feelings of oneness with others. When they consciously acknowledge the presence of these feelings, they begin the initial stage of the spiritual path known as Little Chelaship.

The second phrase is "if there the fire burns bright, warming his brother yet heating not himself." If aspirants perceive that they have genuine concerns for the welfare of other human beings rather than for themselves, they become aware of cleavage or contradiction between these feelings of oneness and their self-centered behavior. Because the sensed cleavage produces psychological problems — discomfort, frustration, and nervous distress — aspirants are brought to a point of inner crisis. When facing this crisis, it would be helpful if they accepted the following premises: First, their psychological difficulties are not unique and are faced by everyone who passes on to the spiritual path. Second, these difficulties indicate progress and opportunity, rather than disaster and failure. And third, the power to produce the needed integration, ending the sensed cleavage, lies within themselves.[3]

The third phrase is "the hour has come for making application to stand before the door." After consciously recognizing the existence of cleavage between lower and higher aspects of themselves, aspirants are ready to begin making application of an intelligent bridging process consisting of self-discipline and self-purification. Their objective is to express inclusive love through their outer behavior, enabling their psychological distress to be resolved through integration rather than suppression. This objective is equivalent to attaining the first initiation and is symbolized by a door for two reasons. First, a door permits entrance into a larger area. After attaining the first initiation, aspirants will enter into a sphere of wider activity because their relationships will be more extensive and satisfying. And second, a door is a discrete threshold. Each aspirant will attain the first initiation at a discrete moment in time, after sufficiently mastering the lessons encountered on the path of probation.

Rule Two

When application has been made in triple form, then let the disciple withdraw that application, and forget it has been made.[4]

During the stage of Little Chelaship, aspirants have a selfish spiritual purpose, such as a vague desire for personal liberation from inner conflicts, for personal integrity, and for personal lasting happiness. They have no true unselfish desire to serve others. During the first part of this stage, they investigate various psychological and spiritual teachings, and they run from one teacher to another according to inclination, opportunity, and necessity. It is important that each aspirant transcend this period of itinerancy, gradually settle down with a single teacher or teaching, and learn to apply a discipline of self-purification.[5]

Impurities are associated with each of the four bodies that constitute the personality. Although most people try to keep their dense physical bodies clean, an aspirant needs to be concerned with impurities associated with the deeper aspects of the personality: illusion on the mental level, glamour on the emotional level, and maya on the etheric level.

Illusion is defined as the power of some mental thought-form to dominate and distort thinking. Such a thoughtform could be based on traditional beliefs from the past, an idea from a current ideology, or a dimly sensed idea that will become popular in the future. Whenever we have a real grasp of the whole idea, there can be no illusion. But if we wrongly perceive, wrongly interpret, or wrongly appropriate the idea, then it can become a narrow and separative ideal, resulting in illusion. Because of illusion, we become fanatics, enforcers of narrow ideals, and limited visionaries.

Glamour is defined as an emotional reaction that prevents clear perception. Its effect is similar to a fog that distorts everything we see or contact, preventing us from viewing the surrounding conditions as they essentially are. Because glamour enters the mind through familiar habits of thought, it is frequently present; because of the nature of emotional reactions, it is powerful; and by being able to masquerade as the truth, it is subtle. For instance, glamour is present whenever we have pride, self-pity, or criticism.

The Sanskrit word *maya* means "illusion," but this word is given a special meaning in the context being considered here. Whereas glamour is illusion that has been intensified by desire, maya is glamour that has been intensified by vital energy. For instance, maya is present whenever we have a compulsion — an irrational repetitive behavior that is difficult to resist. Examples of compulsions include pathological gambling, various eating disturbances, excessive hand-washing, and such sexual disorders as fetishism and voyeurism.

Let us now interpret the second rule. The first phrase is "when application has been made in triple form." When aspirants have applied *self-appointed* rules to themselves, they have taken another step toward simplifying their lives, integrating their personalities, and working efficiently in the world with accuracy and one-pointedness. Application of the rules needs to be made in triple form: dispelling mental illusion, dissipating emotional glamour, and devitalizing etheric maya.

The second phrase is "then let the disciple withdraw that application." A basic law of the universe, sometimes called the Law of Periodicity, states that all evolutionary growth is characterized by rhythm, ebb and flow, and cycles. This law is applicable to all forms in nature, including the solar system, the various kingdoms of nature, and the daily life of an individual human being. The point is that the effort of character building should also be periodic. Spiritual initiation cannot be accomplished in one furious continuous stretch of rushing forth to work, nor can it be accomplished in one eternal siesta. Thus, aspirants have to achieve the wisdom of knowing when it is time to apply self-discipline and when it is time to withdraw that application. If they develop as desired, each period of withdrawal is succeeded by a cycle of greater activity and of more potent achievement.[6]

The third phrase is "and forget it has been made." One should do one's best to complete the active and passive phases of the current cycle of work. Then one should begin a new cycle, forgetting about the previous effort: experiencing neither pride over what was done nor depression due to any lack of accomplishment. However, if aspirants ignore this injunction, they may take pride in being able to adhere to a self-imposed discipline and feel superior to those who are not so disciplined. They may then make self-discipline their goal, confusing the means with the ends and becoming fanatical. Such confusion would increase their sense of separateness, even though the overall objective of the path of probation is to become more inclusive.

Rule Three

Triple the call must be, and long it takes to sound it
forth. Let the disciple sound the cry across the desert,

over the sea, and through the fires which separate him from the veiled and hidden door.[7]

The first three rules present different aspects of a single process of training. The first rule describes the training objective. The second rule describes the cyclic nature of the process, the context in which all work should be done. The third rule describes how the discipline of self-purification should be applied during the active portion of each cycle.

For either an individual, a group, or a kingdom of nature, consciousness unfolds through a series of ascensions. These ascensions are the result of a method of invocation by the lesser entity, followed by the evocation of a factor that is greater, more inclusive, and more enlightened. The lesser entity invokes the greater, and the greater factor responds according to the degree of understanding and dynamic tension displayed by the lesser one. The task of the lesser entity is invocative, and the success of the invocative rite is called evocation. According to Bailey, "The definition of religion which will in the future prove of greater accuracy than any yet formulated by the theologians might be expressed as follows: Religion is the name given to the invocative appeal of humanity and the evocative response of the greater Life to that cry."[8] Invocation and evocation can be thought of as being a science, and Bailey predicts that this science will someday take the place of what is called prayer and worship.[9]

In the case of an aspirant on the path of probation, the effort is to create a point of invocative tension in the personality, which then evokes the attention of the soul. As a result, the vibrations of the personality and soul slowly become reciprocally stronger, until there is a contact between them. The third rule describes this process, and the symbols have the following meanings: "The call" refers to an invocation for purification; "cry," to the responding evocation; "desert," to physical life; "sea," to emotional life; "fires," to mental life; "him," to the aspirant; and "veiled and hidden door," to the first initiation.

According to the first sentence of the rule, the aspirant must invoke new patterns of behavior, feeling, and thinking ("triple the call must be"), and these invocations must be made over a relatively long period ("and long it takes to sound it forth"). Through these invocations, the inner spiritual nature is evoked, enabling it to emerge into manifestation. This evocation can be thought of as a process of unveiling: Each body of the personality is successively brought to a point where it is simply a transparency, permitting the full shining forth of the inner spiritual nature.

The aspirant's first task is to express evoked patterns of behavior across the physical plane ("let the disciple sound the cry across the desert"). The dense physical body is only an automaton, obedient to the controlling forces in the etheric body. Is outer behavior to be controlled by emotional force, producing desire for the gratification of physical appetites and emotional desires? Is it to be responsive to the mind and work under the impulse of projected thought? Or is it to be directed by an energy greater than these, the energy of the soul? The process of evoking new patterns of behavior is based on distinguishing between the spiritual self, which expresses only virtues, and the not-self, which expresses only vices. There are three steps: First, through refusing to be identified with anything regarded as the not-self, become indifferent toward any impulsive irrational behavior but without fighting or placing any concentration on that behavior. Second, through constant recollection of the truth of being the spiritual self, call forth right thought and true idealism from the mind and soul. Third, by projecting the evoked energies down into the etheric body, express new patterns of behavior in the physical world.[10]

The second task is expressing evoked rhythms over the emotional life ("over the sea"). As pointed out by psychologists and physicians, it is a serious mistake to resort to a process of direct suppression of undesirable feelings. Such suppression dams up energy in the solar plexus chakra and could lead to various nervous disorders. It could also lead to cancer of the stomach, the liver, and sometimes the entire abdominal area. Instead of suppression, what is being proposed here is a process of substitution through evocation: Remove attention from self-centered feelings, call in the higher rhythms of the soul, and then allow those new harmonizing rhythms to supersede the restless reactions of the personality. Through expressing the evoked rhythms in the emotional body, it is possible to love collectively and purely, rather than being actuated by personality attraction and the motive of reward. In other words, one becomes group-conscious, sensitive to group ideals, and inclusive in plans and concepts.[11]

The third task is expressing evoked ideas through the mind ("through the fires"), which can be done in the following ways: relegating certain preconceived ideas to the background so that new horizons can be visioned and new ideas can enter; not permitting certain lines of thought and replacing those lines with constructive, creative thinking; reading deeply and widely with the intent to serve others through the material being learned; and cultivating *beauty* in thought, which involves being vitally useful to others and invoking spiritual ideas from the soul. These precepts require a persistent watchfulness over the processes of the mind until the old thought habits have been overcome and the new habits established. Then it will be discovered that the new ideas are sufficiently attractive to focus the thinking of the mind. The old thought patterns will fail to arrest the attention and will die of inanition.[12]

The application of self-discipline is important because impurities in the physical, emotional, and mental bodies separate the aspirant from attaining the first initiation ("which separate him from the veiled and hidden door"). When the desert of physical plane life blossoms like a rose, when the restless waters of the emotional life become still and mirror the indwelling divinity, and when the fiery furnace of the mind is brought under control, then nothing can keep the door of initiation from opening.

Rule Four

Let the disciple tend the evolution of the fire; nourish
the lesser lives, and thus keep the wheel revolving.[13]

The purpose of the preceding rule is to invoke the energies
of the soul so that they can supersede and dominate those of the
personality. This reorientation can be understood in terms of
the chakras. The diaphragm is a muscular partition that separates the abdominal cavity from the chest cavity. The chakras
below the diaphragm control the personality, and the ones
above this partition respond automatically to the inspiration of
the soul. If the impulses and tendencies of the lower self are the
only motivating forces in daily affairs, then the only active
chakras are the lower ones. But if the energies of the soul are
also motivating forces, then the chakras above the diaphragm
are also active. Thus, one effect of the preceding rule is to
increase the activity of the higher chakras.[14]

When aspirants shift the emphasis of their intention from
below to above the diaphragm, in the sense that their higher
chakras govern their behavior more than half of the time, they
enter the second stage on the path of probation, which is called
Chela in the Light. Afterward, they need to continue the previous training and progressively add the new practices
described in rules Four through Seven.

In the fourth rule, the word "wheel" refers to the great
Wheel of Rebirth. The entire human kingdom is symbolized as
being arranged in different positions around this wheel. One
position corresponds to individuals who are being born. Other
positions correspond to children, adolescents, adults, people
who are dying, people in the after-death condition, and people
preparing themselves for rebirth. At any given orientation of the
wheel, one group of human beings is swept into incarnation and
another group is swept out of incarnation. As the wheel turns,
each group progressively experiences the various stages of the
reincarnation cycle.[15] With regard to the other symbols in this
rule, "the fire" refers to the energies of the sacral and solar plexus

chakras, and "lesser lives" refers to human beings needing assistance.

The fourth rule consists of three phrases. The first phrase is "let the disciple tend the evolution of the fire." Aspirants should tend to two processes that transfer energies from centers below the diaphragm to ones above. Before the path of probation, they began the long process of transmuting sexual or physical creativity into artistic or mental creativity, which has the effect of transferring the energy of the sacral chakra to the throat chakra. During the stage of Little Chelaship, they continued that process and began a second long one: transmuting personal desire into group consciousness, which has the effect of transferring the energy of the solar plexus chakra to the heart chakra. Through persistence with these transferences, the throat and heart chakras are brought into activity, and the aspirants enter the stage of Chela in the Light. As a result, they are creatively intelligent along some line and are slowly becoming group-conscious. But because many of their reactions are still selfishly motivated, they need to continue transmuting their sexual and emotional natures.[16]

With regard to transmuting sexuality, aspirants often err in two ways: either stamping out natural sexual desire and enforcing celibacy or trying to exhaust sexual desire through promiscuity and perversion. At certain times, it may be advisable for them to gain control over themselves through a temporary abstention, but that is only a means to an end. True transmutation occurs by having a correct sense of proportion. When there is recognition of the proper place that sex should play in daily life, coupled with attention focused in some area of artistic or mental creativity, the throat chakra automatically becomes magnetic and attracts the forces of the sacral chakra upward through the spine. Through this transference, aspirants can learn to express their sexual lives in a normal and natural way, regulate their sexual activities according to the customs of the land, and set examples to others of spiritual living and moral rectitude.[17]

The second phrase is "nourish the lesser lives." Because of their growing group consciousness, aspirants become motivated to nourish other human beings through service. However, they should learn to render impersonal service, rather than an emotional insistence on handling the affairs of others. Impersonal service is a definite technique of spiritual integration; it evokes the soul powers and continues the process of transferring the energy of the solar plexus chakra to the heart chakra. Learning to serve in an impersonal way involves answering two questions prior to any activity: Is my motive a spiritual impulse, or am I being prompted by emotion, ambition to shine, and love of being loved or admired? Am I providing this service as an individual to an individual, or am I giving it as a member of a group to a group?[18]

The third phrase is "thus keep the wheel revolving." During the stage of Chela in the Light, aspirants are able to perceive the material needs of people and respond to those needs, but they are not yet ready to help with the spiritual evolution of others. For instance, they may be involved in welfare movements, philanthropic endeavors, Red Cross work, educational improvements, and hospices. The great Wheel of Rebirth depicts the cycle of changes in the personality life of human beings, not changes in the spiritual life. Through their service, aspirants help to keep the Wheel of Rebirth revolving, in the sense of helping someone take the next step in the cyclic progression of personality activity. In contrast, on the path of discipleship, disciples learn to perceive and meet the spiritual needs of people, helping them to establish contact with their souls, stand in spiritual being, and leave the Wheel of Rebirth.[19]

Rule Five

Let the applicant see to it that the solar angel dims the light of the lunar angels, remaining the sole luminary in the microcosmic sky.[20]

The will-to-love is the intention to express right relation-ships throughout the world, starting with oneself and one's immediate associates. Through application of the previous rule, aspirants gradually intensify their will-to-love. However, they also observe that they lack love, often feeling isolated from and not identified with other people, feeling superior to their associates and being irritated by them, and thinking that others are presenting handicaps to their own expression of love. In their highest and best moments, they make a laborious effort to be nice, to refrain from uttering the things that their critical minds say, and to avoid acting on the opinions they may have formed. However, they also know the difference between a truly spontaneous love in action and their strenuous effort to display a theory of love.[21]

The stimulation of their growing will-to-love leads aspi-rants to discover the vices that they express and the virtues that they need to acquire. The terms *virtue* and *vice*, as used here, do not refer to conforming to various man-made laws and social customs. Instead, these terms refer to one's attitude toward oneself and other people. A virtue is a manifestation of the spirit of cooperation with others, and a vice is the opposite of that attitude. A virtue calls in the vibratory rhythm of group consciousness and enables the love aspect of the soul to become the motivating factor. A vice is an expression of a separative impulse that subordinates the soul to the goals of the lower self. For instance, virtues include forgiveness, tenderness, humility, tolerance, patience, compassion, serenity, and wide-mindedness. On the other hand, vices include qualities such as resentment, hardness, pride, arrogance, willfulness, contempt, worrying, and bigotry.[22]

After identifying the virtues they need to acquire, aspi-rants must next learn to display those virtues. One way of manifesting a particular virtue is to reflect deeply and con-stantly on the significance and meaning of that virtue, includ-ing its origin, qualities, goals, and objectives. Another way is through visualization, which is the approach described by the fifth rule.

The symbols in the fifth rule have the following interpretations: "The solar angel" refers to an image of oneself as expressing virtues; "lunar angel," to an image of oneself as expressing vices; and "microcosmic sky," to the inner field of visualization.

The recommended approach for using visualization is as follows: Start by imagining yourself as the exponent of the virtue you desire most, and then add virtue to virtue until you have included all of the virtues ("let the applicant see to it"). Use the creative imagination of the emotional body to picture the desired form, and use the thought energy of the mind to give life and direction to that form. When working effectively, you can construct a rapport or line of energy between the emotional body and mind. As a result, the image of yourself expressing virtues dims the influence of all opposing self-images still present in your memory ("that the solar angel dims the light of the lunar angels"). During the rest of the day, ensure that this positive image remains the sole picture of yourself within your inner field of visualization ("remaining the sole luminary in the microcosmic sky"), enabling you to become that image in daily life.[23]

This rule is based on the Biblical proverb, "For as he thinketh in his heart, so is he" (Proverbs 23:7). The heart is the custodian of the power of the imagination. Unconsciously or consciously, we are always creating self-images based on what we think about ourselves and what we feel ourselves to be. Afterward, our power of imagination manifests those images in our outer experiences. Generally, this process is unconscious, but the purpose of the fifth rule is to make it conscious.

Rule Six

The purificatory fires burn dim and low when the third is sacrificed to the fourth. Therefore let the dis-

ciple refrain from taking life, and let him nourish that
which is lowest with the produce of the second.[24]

Because of their steadily growing will-to-love, aspirants
become interested in learning additional ways to increase their
expression of love. According to the sixth rule, one such way is
to become a vegetarian. Since this rule refers to the kingdoms
of nature, it may be helpful to review some information about
them.

Four kingdoms of nature are present in the physical
world: the first is the mineral, the second is the vegetable, the
third is the animal, and the fourth is the human. Each kingdom
draws sustenance from the ones that have preceded it during
the evolutionary process. For instance, the vegetable kingdom
draws its vital strength from the sun, water, and the mineral
content of the earth. The animal kingdom draws its sustenance
primarily from the sun, water, and the vegetable kingdom.
The mineral content needed for the animal's skeleton structure
is taken from the vegetable kingdom, rather than directly from
the ground. The human kingdom follows the same procedure
and draws its sustenance from the sun, water, vegetable kingdom, and animal kingdom. Thus, it is not intrinsically evil for
human beings to eat animal meat. At an early stage of human
evolution, animal meat can be a right and proper food.[25]

The symbols in the sixth rule have the following interpretations: "the purificatory fires" refers to inclusive love; "third,"
to the third (animal) kingdom; "fourth," to the fourth (human)
kingdom; "lowest," to the physical body; and "second," to the
second (vegetable) kingdom.

Different foods carry different qualities or vibrations. Our
awareness of the essential unity of humanity, which is inclusive
love, diminishes and becomes less apparent when animal meat
is eaten by us ("the purificatory fires burn dim and low when
the third is sacrificed to the fourth"). This type of food tends to
reinforce material or animal characteristics such as physical
appetites and strong emotional desires, which in turn reinforce

identification with physical form. Therefore, we should refrain from eating foods that require the taking of animal life ("therefore let the disciple refrain from taking life") because those foods are qualified by the intense emotions experienced by the animals when they are being slaughtered. However, we can still eat animal products that do not require the taking of life, such as eggs, cheese, milk, and butter. On the other hand, eating fruits, nuts, grains, and vegetables helps to reinforce spiritual qualities. Thus, as much as possible, we should nourish our physical bodies with the produce of the vegetable kingdom ("and let him nourish that which is lowest with the produce of the second").

With regard to this rule, it is important to display common sense. We should be aware of the conditions in our environment and always maintain an appropriate and balanced combination of foods in our diet. Being physically healthy while eating meat is better than becoming sick by adhering to a rigid vegetarian diet. It is also important to move slowly when making dietary changes, recognizing that everything in nature moves slowly. For instance, rather than permanently giving up certain kinds of foods, we may wish to experiment with fasting, which means abstaining from those foods for only limited periods of time.[26]

Rule Seven

Let the disciple turn his attention to the enunciating of those sounds which echo in the halls where walks the Master. Let him not sound the lesser notes which awaken vibration within the halls of Maya.[27]

The seventh rule is the final one for the path of probation, and it provides the most advanced instruction. By working with the preceding rules, aspirants have strengthened their belief in having a soul, which they may think of as being the

inner voice of God within the mind. They also have strengthened their belief in being able to receive guidance from this
inner source of wisdom. However, until they are close to the
end of the path of probation, they feel that their comprehension
regarding the soul is still incomplete. As a result, they do not
rely on the soul's guidance for obtaining solutions to their most
difficult and pressing problems. Instead, they wrestle with
those problems in an emotional way with anxiety, worry, eva-
sion, and defensive suppressions. Since an emotional approach
cannot be successful, their subconscious minds remain bewil-
dered with unsolved problems: a half-realized inability to work
out right relations with people, fretting and gnawing at the
lower layers of unformulated thought, and resentment against
life, people, and past decisions.

Nevertheless, some aspirants eventually reach a stage in
their evolution when they are ready to assume that they comprehend and are willing to act on that comprehended knowledge. The seventh rule corresponds to that stage and describes
the *as if* technique: the constant attempt to live *as if* the soul is
in control and is dominating the personality. The phrase *as if*
means that those aspirants are not fully convinced that the soul
either exists or is in control, but they are willing to live their
lives as though this circumstance were true.[28]

The symbols in the seventh rule have the following meanings: "those sounds" refers to thoughts and speech; "halls," to
physical behavior; "Master," to the soul; "vibration," to a habit
pattern; and "Maya," to ignorance of the soul.

When you are ready to rely on the guidance of the soul,
turn your attention to learning the *as if* technique ("let the
disciple turn his attention"). This technique has two different
phases. In the active phase, express thoughts and speech that
echo in your physical behavior as if you are walking humbly
with the soul ("to the enunciating of those sounds which echo in
the halls where walks the Master"). In other words, act as if the
soul, or inner voice of God, is always accompanying you on
your life's journey, as if the soul is always revealing the next

step that should be taken, as if that guidance can be received simply by listening for it, and as if the soul's guidance is the master of your life.

The passive phase of the technique is meditative reflection. During this phase, think carefully about the soul and its relationship to the personality. Reflect also on the changes that need to be made in your personality so that your thoughts and speech do not awaken or reinforce patterns of behavior based on ignorance of the soul ("let him not sound the lesser notes which awaken vibration within the halls of Maya"). For instance, you might reflect on the following questions: When truly thinking as if your mind were the instrument of the soul, what lines of thought would have to be eliminated, cultivated, or expressed? When realistically living as if the soul were visible in daily life, what would be happening in your emotional body? When the *as if* technique is controlling your physical brain and consequently your daily activities, in what way would your mode of living be altered?[29]

The *as if* technique is a cyclic process. For the periods of activity to be eloquent and productive, there must be balancing periods of quiet reflection. The two sentences in the seventh rule characterize both phases of the technique. By implementing both phases, we can establish a rhythm of activity and meditation. By maintaining this rhythm so that it becomes a spiritual habit, we can develop an instinctual spiritual responsiveness to the challenges of life, automatically saying and doing the right things.

It is important to understand the difference between the fifth rule and the *as if* technique. The fifth rule is based on the Biblical proverb "For as he thinketh in his heart, so is he," and it brings about the imposition of mental control upon the personality. In contrast, the *as if* technique is based on another Biblical proverb: "Walk humbly with thy God" (Micah 6:8). This technique brings in the will aspect of the soul, which can then operate through the powers of thought and imagination.[30]

Chapter 2

Elementary Rules for Meditation

Human evolution proceeds as a series of integrations. Before we are ready to tread the spiritual path, we must accomplish the following integrations: between the dense physical body and the etheric, or, vital body; between these two and the emotional body; between these three and the mental body; and between these four and the personality as a whole. On the spiritual path, we learn to accomplish higher integrations: between the coordinated personality and the soul and between the soul-infused personality and the spirit. *Meditation* can be defined as a process of increasing the sensitivity of the lower integrated aspects to that higher aspect that is next to be integrated. An appropriate method of meditation exists for us at any point of our evolution, and that method changes as we evolve.

Each symbol in each of Bailey's rules has two different interpretations. The preceding chapter interpreted the symbols in the first seven rules as describing a sevenfold process of character building for the path of probation. This chapter

interprets those same symbols as describing a sevenfold process
of meditation for the path of probation. The latter process has
two divisions. Rules One through Three give instruction on
meditation for the first stage, Little Chelaship, and rules Four
through Seven give instruction for the second stage, Chela in
the Light.

Rule One

Let the disciple search within the heart's deep cave. If
there the fire burns bright, warming his brother yet
heating not himself, the hour has come for making
application to stand before the door.[1]

To understand this rule, it is necessary to review some
additional concepts regarding esoteric anatomy. According to
various writers in both yoga and theosophy, the etheric spine
consists of three channels with the Sanskrit names *sushumna*,
pingala, and *ida*. The central channel is sushumna, and pingala
and ida are on the sides. *Kundalini* is a Sanskrit word meaning
the "sleeping divine power at the base of the spine." The kundalini energy, sometimes called the "fire of matter," emanates
from the basic chakra. It uses the pingala channel and has the
ability to stimulate the major etheric chakras. Two other
etheric energies can also flow through these spinal channels.
The "fire of manas" emanates from the throat chakra. It uses
the ida channel and improves sensitivity to impressions. The
"fire of spirit" emanates from the crown chakra. It uses the
sushumna channel and embodies energies from the soul.[2]

An interlaced web of etheric substance, disk-shaped, lies
between each pair of major chakras. When intact, these etheric
webs impede the free flow of energies in the etheric body.
Through the practices of character building and meditation,
these webs are slowly and automatically dissipated. Each spiritual initiation corresponds to the opening of one of these webs,

resulting in an increased passage of energy and attainment of a higher state of consciousness.[3]

The average intelligent citizen, predominately controlled by his or her lower nature, has already dissipated the two lowest webs, leaving the higher webs still intact. The first initiation corresponds to opening the web lying between the solar plexus and heart chakra, which allows the kundalini energy to reach and stimulate the heart chakra. The second initiation corresponds to opening the web lying between the heart chakra and throat chakra, enabling the kundalini energy to reach and stimulate the throat, brow, and crown chakras. Before the third initiation, the kundalini is regarded as "sleeping," even though this energy may be actively stimulating the higher chakras. The third initiation corresponds to opening the web lying between the throat chakra and brow chakra, enabling the fire of manas to reach and stimulate the brow and crown chakras. Afterward, the three fires of matter, manas, and spirit can be unified in the basic chakra and then be raised up through the threefold spine to stimulate further the higher chakras. This union of the three fires is sometimes called the "awakened" kundalini.

The first rule describes some prerequisites for practicing meditation, and it also describes the objective of meditation for the path of probation. The symbols have the following meanings: "the heart's deep cave" refers to the etheric spinal column; "fire burns bright," to vitality and alertness; "brother," to the personality; "making application," to practicing meditation; and "door," to the soul.

Let us now interpret each phrase in the first rule. Before beginning to meditate, you should investigate the condition of your etheric spinal column connecting the heart chakra with the basic chakra ("let the disciple search within the heart's deep cave"). Because the etheric body is below the threshold of consciousness, the condition of the etheric spinal column is generally recognized only in terms of vitality and alertness, or the lack of these qualities.

If you sense that vitality and alertness are present, indicating that the kundalini energy from the basic chakra is active ("if there the fire burns bright"), then you have met the first prerequisite for meditation. Why is this prerequisite important? When people quiet their minds by suppressing the movement of thought, they may retard their development and stultify their progress. All beginners use suppression to some extent until they learn to guard against it. Instead, achieve placidity of mind by raising the vibration of consciousness as high as possible and keeping it there. As long as this vibration is the same as that of the soul on its own plane, the mind will be held in a state of equilibrium without detrimental effects. The point is that the desired condition can be attained only when vitality and alertness are present. To meet this prerequisite, avoid practicing meditation when feeling tired, fatigued, or ill. The best time is early in the morning before having breakfast because the process of digestion can also be an interference. In addition, have sufficient sleep and contact with the sun, and eat only pure foods that provide vitalization, such as milk, honey, whole-wheat bread, all vegetables that contact the sun, oranges, bananas, raisins, nuts, potatoes, and unpolished rice.[4]

In any series of instruction having a truly esoteric nature, one of the main teachings concerns the *attitude* of the student toward the lower bodies. According to the next phrase in the rule, the second prerequisite for meditation is having the attitude that the etheric body is energizing the personality but not the real or spiritual self ("warming his brother yet heating not himself"). In other words, acknowledge being a spiritual entity, different from the lower bodies with respect to nature, objectives, and methods of working. For instance, think of the personality as similar to a suit of clothes, something that can be temporarily occupied and worn but that is certainly not yourself.[5]

If an active kundalini and right attitude are present, then the time has come for making application of the rules for meditation discussed in this chapter ("the hour has come for making application"). The objective of these rules is to raise the vibration of consciousness until it reaches that of the soul ("to stand before the door"). In the final phrase of the first rule, the soul is symbolized by a door. When you stand in consciousness before that door, it will open and allow intuitive ideas to flow into your mind.

After the vibration of consciousness is raised by applying the rules in this chapter, the kundalini energy will eventually and automatically rise further along the etheric spine, tearing the web lying between the solar plexus and heart chakra. However, there are systems of occultism that deliberately attempt to raise the kundalini without first raising consciousness. These methods, sometimes called kundalini yoga, are based on exercising conscious control over interior energies, plus utilizing special postures, breathing exercises, and muscle contractions. When successful, which is not very often, kundalini yoga causes premature burning and destruction of the etheric webs. As a result, the brain cells can become overstimulated, possibly leading to insanity or brain tumors. The etheric webs actually have a beneficent function: They prevent our chakras from receiving more energies than we have wisdom, purification, and physical condition to handle. Thus, the reader is strongly advised to avoid all systems of meditation that deliberately attempt to raise the kundalini energy or to tear the etheric webs.[6]

Rule Two

When application has been made in triple form, then let the disciple withdraw that application, and forget it has been made.[7]

According to the ancient Hindu tradition, a person's first stage in life is that of a student; the second stage is that of a householder; and the third stage is withdrawal from family and business, retiring in the forest to find spiritual truth. Today, although the call for withdrawal remains the same, we need not leave behind our familiar environment and outer usefulness. We can remain right where we happen to be, continuing to fulfill our outer duties. The only withdrawal we must make is from our agelong identification with form life. Assagioli has emphasized the importance of this type of withdrawal: "We are dominated by everything with which our self becomes identified. We can dominate and control everything from which we dis-identify ourselves."[8]

What does it mean to be identified with form life? People tend to identify with anything that gives them pleasure or to which they give importance. For instance, a woman entering a beauty contest identifies with her physical body and its attractiveness. A professional athlete identifies with his muscular strength and control. Some individuals may identify with their emotional life, perhaps with their roles as wife, husband, mother, or father. And other people may identify with their mental life and take pride in their ability to think, argue, or explain.

The Sanskrit word *raja* means "kingly." Raja yoga, one of the traditional systems of self-development devised in India, is considered to be kingly because of the power and wisdom that are conferred. *Pratyahara* means "self-withdrawal" and is a preliminary step in raja yoga. It includes withdrawing from identification with form life, disengaging the self from unthinking attachment to the not-self, and centering the consciousness within the head.[9] Pratyahara has three steps, each of which is described by a phrase in the second rule.

The first phrase is "when application has been made in triple form." Pratyahara begins with the deliberate application of a dis-identification exercise to three fields of observation: sensations, feelings, and thoughts. The approach discriminates actively between the inner self, or pure consciousness, and the fields that are the contents of consciousness. The first field is that of physical sensations produced by bodily conditions, such as comfort, fatigue, hunger, warmth, and so on. Through calm observation of those sensations, discover two reasons for dis-identifying with the physical body: Physical sensations are transitory, fleeting, and often contradictory, whereas the inner self has stability and permanence; and those sensations can be observed, whereas the inner self is the observer. Because of agelong identification with the physical body, it is helpful to affirm the following with conviction: "I have a body, but I am not my body."

This dis-identification exercise is similar to peeling off the various layers of an onion. After considering physical sensations, investigate the field of emotions or feelings, such as desire, fear, hope, and irritation. By recognizing that feelings are countless, contradictory, and changing, and that they can be observed, understood, and then dominated, realize the difference between the emotional body and the inner self. To aid in withdrawing from identification with the emotional body, affirm with conviction: "I have feelings, but I am not my feelings." The final field of observation is that of mental activity, such as having various thoughts, beliefs, concepts, attitudes, and ideas. Because the inner self can observe, take notice of, develop, and discipline the mind, realize that the self is not the mind. Here it is helpful to affirm: "I have an intellect, but I am not my intellect."[10]

The second phrase in the rule is "then let the disciple withdraw that application." By completing the foregoing exercise, you will discover that there is an Observer who observes the succession of sensations, feelings, and thoughts. Next, withdraw the effort of dis-identifying with the not-self and instead deliberately identify with the true self: the inner Observer, Perceiver, and Actor. To aid in this step, it is helpful to say another affirmation. Bailey suggests, for example, the reiterated appreciation of the following words: "I am the Self, the Self am I."[11] As another example, Assagioli suggests saying: "I recognize and affirm that I am a Centre of pure self-consciousness. I am a Centre of Will, capable of mastering, directing and using all my psychological processes and my physical body."[12]

The third phrase is "and forget it has been made." Through deliberate dis-identification with the personality and then deliberate identification with the inner Observer, you will automatically raise your consciousness to a point within the region of the pituitary and pineal glands inside your head. From that central position you can carry out the final step of pratyahara, which is observing your personality in a detached way. However, to be fully observant during the immediate moment, forget all affirmations made during the earlier two steps because reiterating those statements is a distraction. Instead, simply observe what is actually taking place both inside and outside the personality without any justification, reaction, or defensiveness.

Pratyahara is the first technique of meditation that must be learned on the path of probation, and it is a prerequisite for all later techniques. Aspirants should develop the habit of practicing the steps of pratyahara at least once a day, preferably early in the morning. By developing this habit, they can gain control over those psychological contents with which they were previously identified, protect themselves against the constant stream of influences that try to manipulate and dominate them, find a new sense of freedom and enhanced being, develop a greater ability to maintain the attitude of self-observation during the rest of the day, and prepare themselves for more advanced work in meditation.

Rule Three

Triple the call must be, and long it takes to sound it forth. Let the disciple sound the cry across the desert, over the sea, and through the fires which separate him from the veiled and hidden door.[13]

Through application of the preceding rule, aspirants learn to observe their behavior in an objective way. After encountering facets of themselves that they did not previously realize or acknowledge, they awaken to the need of gaining a reasonable and truthful understanding of the motives that underlie their activities. The third rule gives instruction for this new effort. Before interpreting the symbols, it is necessary to consider a series of philosophical definitions.

A human being consists of a personality, a soul, and a spirit. Each of these components can be divided into three aspects. The personality includes the physical (both the dense and etheric), emotional, and mental bodies. The soul includes the qualities of wisdom, love, and will. And the spirit, sometimes called the spiritual triad, includes the spiritual mind, spiritual love, and spiritual will.

The mental plane consists of seven subplanes that are divided into two groups: the lowest four subplanes are the concrete levels, and the top three subplanes are the abstract levels. An individual has three focal points of perception on these subplanes. One focal point is *the mental body*—sometimes called the concrete mind or simply the mind—which is composed of matter from the lowest four subplanes. The mental body is the highest aspect of the personality and is concerned with knowledge or concrete thoughts. Another focal point of perception is *the soul*—sometimes called the causal body or egoic lotus—which consists of matter from the second and third divisions (counting from the top) of the mental plane. The soul is the storehouse for wisdom, which is the abstracted essence gained from a person's experience, and it is the instrument for expressing principles or abstract thoughts. The third focal point, *the spiritual mind*, is the lowest aspect of the spiritual triad, and it is composed of matter from only the highest mental subplane. The spiritual mind can convey insights, or direct perceptions of truth, that reflect the innate divine nature with clarity, synthesis, and inclusiveness. After receiving insights from the spiritual mind, the soul can use those insights to guide its own expression of abstract thinking, which in turn can guide the concrete thinking of the mental body.[14]

The Sanskrit word *guna* means "quality." According to Hindu philosophy, everything in nature is composed of three gunas: *tamas*, *rajas*, and *sattva*. The Sanskrit word *tamas* means "inertia," and it represents dullness, inaction, ignorance, incapacity, darkness, and obscurity. The word *rajas* means "restlessness" and represents passion, action, struggle, effort, and the thirst of desire. The word *sattva* means "serenity and harmony"; it represents goodness, purity, balance, happiness, light, and virtue.

For instance, each kingdom of nature has a predominating guna. Working blindly, without being able to respond consciously to the environment, subhuman lives express the guna of tamas. By being involved in constant and conscious change, human lives demonstrate the guna of rajas. And by responding harmoniously to the divine urge, superhuman lives express the guna of sattva.[15]

In the third rule, the symbols have the following meanings: "the call" refers to the invocation of thoughts, wisdom, and insights; "cry," to the evoked understanding; "across the desert," to having a material perspective; "over the sea," to being activated by emotional energy; "through the fires," to expressing soul energy through the mind; "him," to the vibration of consciousness; and "the veiled and hidden door," to the soul.

To discover your underlying motives, apply a process of invocation and evocation. After raising your consciousness to the head, as described in the second rule, invoke insights from the spiritual mind, wisdom or abstract thoughts from the soul, and concrete thoughts from the lower concrete mind ("triple the call must be"). The invocation of insights occurs when making the effort to observe directly your sensations, feelings, and thoughts during the immediate moment. The invocation of wisdom occurs when making the effort to organize these observations and uncover the motives that lie behind your outer activities. And the invocation of concrete thoughts occurs when making the effort to relate your motives to the facts of your daily life. Furthermore, it is necessary to make this threefold invocation over a relatively long period ("and long it takes to sound it forth"). For instance, Bailey suggests that a written record concerning this inquiry be kept three times each day for one year.[16]

Understanding can be defined as the synthesis of insights, wisdom, and concrete thoughts. Through making the foregoing invocation, you can evoke understanding ("let the disciple sound the cry") about when you are displaying one of the three gunas: tamas, or having an outlook that is strictly material ("across the desert"); rajas, or being activated by emotional energy ("over the sea"); and sattva, or expressing soul energy through the mind ("and through the fires"). It is important to discover the motivating forces that underlie your activities because those forces are preventing the vibration of your consciousness from rising and reaching that of the soul ("which separate him from the veiled and hidden door").

For instance, if the tamas quality predominates, then you are swayed strongly by physical forces and are involved with "the sins of the flesh" such as gluttony, drink, and licentiousness. If the rajas quality predominates, then you live a potent emotional and psychic life, which may mean that you are overly sensitive, irritable, and impressionable. If the sattva quality predominates, then the forces of the soul are superseding those of the personality. Perhaps, like so many of us, you are swayed by all three types of energy: physical and emotional with an occasional flow of soul energy. In any case, make an honest and objective inventory of the forces that are controlling your life. By applying the rules for character building discussed in the preceding chapter, subordinate the forces that need to be weakened, strengthen the ones that need to be emphasized, and thereby move forward on the path of your destiny.[17]

Rule Four

Let the disciple tend the evolution of the fire; nourish the lesser lives, and thus keep the wheel revolving.[18]

Rules Four through Seven in this chapter give instruction on meditation for the second stage on the path of probation, Chela in the Light. During this stage, aspirants increase their sensitivity in two different directions: to human need, leading to a life of service; and to soul impression, leading to new understanding. The preceding chapter emphasized the first direction; the remaining rules in this chapter emphasize the second direction.

Before interpreting the fourth rule, some additional background information may be helpful. The etheric body is the field of vitality that underlies and controls every part of the dense physical body. Because the chakras are force centers in the etheric body, the aliveness or sluggishness of those centers is responsible for the corresponding activity in the dense physical body. In addition to the seven major chakras listed in Table 1, the etheric body also has twenty-one minor chakras. This book is concerned with only three minor chakras: the splenic chakra and the two centers in the palms of the hands. Many authors count the splenic chakra, instead of the sacral, as one of the seven major chakras.

Prana is a Sanskrit word derived from *pra*, meaning "forth," and the verb root *an*, meaning "to breathe." Thus, prana means "to breathe forth," and it refers to the "life breath" or "life force" that vitalizes the etheric body, which in turn vitalizes the dense physical body. Yogi Ramacharaka gives the following definition: "Prana is the Force by which all activity is carried on in the body—by which all bodily movements are possible—by which all functioning is done—by which all signs of life manifest themselves."[19]

One of the functions of the splenic chakra is to absorb prana from the atmosphere. Afterward, the absorbed prana circulates throughout the etheric body and vitalizes the other chakras. This circulation generally occurs below the threshold of consciousness, which means that it is controlled by the subconscious mind. However, according to the tradition of yoga, the circulation of prana can also be deliberately controlled by the conscious mind. The Sanskrit word *yama* means "regulation" or "control," and the word *pranayama* refers to the deliberate regulation of the flow of prana. As an analogy, such dense physical organs as the heart and stomach generally function automatically below the threshold of consciousness. Nevertheless, according to contemporary biofeedback research, a person can exercise volitional control over these seemingly involuntary organs.[20]

In the fourth rule, the symbols have the following meanings: "the fire" refers to prana; "lesser lives," to the cells and organs composing the dense physical body; and "wheel," to a chakra in the etheric body.

You should learn how to practice pranayama, an exercise that combines three elements: a comfortable physical posture, the rhythm of breathing, and the circulation of prana throughout the etheric body ("let the disciple tend the evolution of the fire"). When done correctly, pranayama provides several benefits. The oxygenating effect of the breathing cleanses the bloodstream, which then nourishes the individual organs and cells in the dense physical body ("nourish the lesser lives"). The rhythm of the exercise is imposed upon the etheric body according to the spacing and counts of the different phases of the breathing cycle. The rhythmic circulation of prana vitalizes each wheel of energy, or chakra ("and thus keep the wheel revolving"). The dense physical body is completely subjugated and brought into line with the etheric body so that the two parts of the physical vehicle form a single integrated unit. Finally, prana is transmitted, via the etheric body, to all parts of the dense physical body.[21]

The effect of pranayama on your chakras depends on the trend of your thoughts. If you have not reached the stage of being a Chela in the Light, then the emphasis of your life lies below the diaphragm, implying that the trend of your thoughts is associated with your lower chakras. Thus, if you practice pranayama before being a Chela in the Light or before even beginning the path of probation, the exercise will stimulate your lower chakras. As a result, you may encounter several undesirable effects, such as overstimulation of your sexual life, strengthening of your emotional nature, awakening a psychic ability before being able to control or understand that ability, and physical disease. On the other hand, when you have reached the stage of being a Chela in the Light, the emphasis of your life has shifted above the diaphragm, and pranayama will stimulate your higher chakras. Thus, in this series of rules on meditation, instruction on pranayama is not given until the stage of Chela in the Light has been reached.[22]

To guard against possible harm when practicing pranayama, remember to apply the preceding rules. As indicated by the first rule, do not practice this exercise when feeling overly tired or ill or after eating. For best results, be rested and in reasonably good health. As indicated by the second rule, remain focused in the head, which means being steady, balanced, alert, and conscious at all times. If you hold your consciousness steady in your head, then pranayama will have the effect of stimulating your crown and brow chakras, thereby strengthening your intuitive nature. As indicated by the third rule, investigate the physical, emotional, and spiritual forces that are motivating influences in your affairs. By making this investigation over an extended period of time, ascertain the particular forces that are being strengthened or weakened by the exercise. If pranayama seems to be having an injurious effect, discontinue the practice.

Different yoga groups teach different forms of pranayama, but they generally do not make this type of instruction available to the general public, limiting it instead to their pledged membership. The reason for the secrecy is that deliberate pranayama can be harmful when done prematurely or incorrectly. The old precept that aspirants must find their way into an esoteric or mystery school is still true. Because careful personal supervision by an experienced teacher is highly desirable, no specific instruction in pranayama is given here.

Pranayama should be done no more than once or twice a day, preferably as preparation for a formal period of meditation. Instruction for the rest of the meditation period is given in the rules that follow. Even if you do not know a pranayama exercise, you can still prepare yourself for meditation by ensuring that your posture is comfortable, upright, and relaxed and that your breathing pattern is quiet and regular.

Rule Five

Let the applicant see to it that the solar angel dims the light of the lunar angels, remaining the sole luminary in the microcosmic sky.[23]

The practice of pratyahara, described in the second rule, raises consciousness to a point within the region of the pituitary and pineal glands inside the head. When consciousness has been raised to that high point, one can be sensitive in three different directions: *outward* upon the world of physical living, *inward* upon the world of emotions and mental perceptions, and *upward* toward the soul. Most people are involved with just receiving impressions from the physical world. During the stage of Little Chelaship, aspirants become interested in uncovering their motives and begin looking in the second direction. During the stage represented by the fifth rule, they develop an additional interest — receiving impressions from the soul, corresponding to looking in the third direction.[24]

The fifth rule describes a receptive form of meditation. Although the purpose of receptive meditation is to increase sensitivity to the soul, this growth in sensitivity is paradoxical. From one point of view, sensitivity cannot be increased through some type of process or ordered training. Aspirants are already sensitive to their souls, but they may not know that when preoccupied with outer matters, form life, and objective things. The approach of receptive meditation is simply to dim the loud assertions of the personality, permitting the light of the soul to pour through.[25]

The symbols have the following meanings in this rule: "solar angel" refers to the intuitive voice of the soul; "lunar angels," to the many voices of the personality; and "microcosmic sky," to the inner field of thought.

The recommended approach for practicing receptive meditation is as follows: Raise the consciousness as high in the head as possible, as described in the second rule. Either practice a pranayama exercise, as described in the fourth rule, or simply establish a correct posture and breathing rhythm. With full concentrated interest and attention, become oriented to the soul ("let the applicant see to it"). Achieve the position of *listening* for the intuitive voice of the soul so that this voice dims the influence of the many voices of the personality ("that the solar angel dims the light of the lunar angels"). Finally, maintain the listening position for the rest of the meditation period, enabling the voice of the soul to remain the sole guiding light within the inner field of thought ("remaining the sole luminary in the microcosmic sky").

When practicing receptive meditation, train yourself in the arduous task of distinguishing between the "lunar angels" and the "solar angel." In particular, it is necessary to discriminate between instinct and intuition, lower and higher mind, desire and spiritual impulse, and selfish aspiration and divine incentive. If you do discern the voice of the soul during the meditation period, be careful to keep an exact record of it. Perhaps this voice comes as the emergence of some clear thought, clarification of some bewilderment, or expansion of some mental perception into intuitive understanding.[26]

Receptive meditation is dualistic in nature because the effort is to receive guidance from a source conceived of as being beyond or higher than oneself. Unfortunately, there is a danger with this type of meditation: If meditators are anxious to receive light from above and have a strong determination to eliminate their thoughts, they may fixate on some thought or image and enter a hypnotic trance. The trance condition is definitely undesirable because the personality is separated from the soul and cannot apprehend the voice of the soul. Although meditators may think they are receiving new and unusual information while in a hypnotic trance, such as during automatic writing or what is now called "channeling," they are probably just extracting the contents of their own subconscious minds. Or, as described in the seventh rule, they may have developed a psychic ability and are receiving information from the astral plane. In either of these cases, a person in a hypnotic trance lacks control over the process and is unable to check the source of the received information.[27]

Therefore, when practicing receptive meditation, it is important to avoid the possibility of a hypnotic trance. In particular, hold the listening position for only as long as you can maintain a recollection of who you are and what you are doing. In the beginning, you may not be able to hold the listening position in the correct way for as long as three minutes, but through practice you can develop the faculty of mind control and be able to hold the position for a much longer time.[28]

Rule Six

The purificatory fires burn dim and low when the third is sacrificed to the fourth. Therefore let the dis-

ciple refrain from taking life, and let him nourish that
which is lowest with the produce of the second.[29]

By applying the fifth rule, Chelas in the Light are able to
receive revelations from their souls. Because these revelations
are concerned with correcting the faults of their personalities,
they tread the way of what is called "the lesser revelation." In
contrast, the greater revelation is concerned with divinity and
its nature. Chelas in the Light eventually receive three important revelations. First, they share all human tendencies, both
good and bad, and thus are able to serve. Second, the things in
others that they most despise and fear are things that they have
strongly inside themselves but have not yet recognized. Third,
dogmatic ways of looking at life and people, such as those
based on religious or national traditions, are useless when those
attitudes separate them from others.[30]

In most of her books, Bailey uses the listing of the chakras
given in Table 1, which includes the crown and brow chakras
as separate centers. However, in the book providing the rules
for initiation that we are now studying, Bailey consistently
refers to the crown and brow centers as though they were two
divisions of a single center called the head center. The enumer-
ation in the sixth rule is based on that same convention.
Because the first chakra is the head center, consisting of both
the crown and brow, the "second" is the throat; the "third" is the
heart; and the "fourth" is the solar plexus. With regard to the
other symbols in this rule, "purificatory fires" refers to the intuitive voice of the soul; and "lowest" refers to the outer behavior
of the personality.

The intuitive voice of the soul burns dim and low when
the inclusive love of the heart chakra is sacrificed for the self-
centered ambition of the solar plexus chakra ("the purificatory
fires burn dim and low when the third is sacrificed to the
fourth"). In other words, when you enter receptive meditation
with self-centered objectives and separative agendas, you lack
rapport with the soul and have difficulty in hearing its voice.

But when you have the objective of manifesting the plan of the soul in your life, you are sensitive to the soul. Therefore, you need to do two things.

First, refrain from having any motive or attitude that would take the synthetic life of humanity away from your awareness ("therefore let the disciple refrain from taking life"). The soul is intrinsically group-conscious. To develop a rapport with the soul, you must become group-conscious also. When you are willing to look at your situation from the vantage point of the whole, you can receive revelations regarding the faults in your character, limitations in your expression, and inadequacies in your conduct.

Second, after receiving such a revelation, make the needed corrections in your outer behavior ("and let him nourish that which is lowest"). An effective way of making these corrections is by projecting affirmations into the etheric body with the aid of the throat chakra ("with the produce of the second"). Affirmations are ideas formulated into clear thought-forms, and they should embody some purpose, planned activity, or recognized goal. For best results, they should be audibly spoken, with the right feeling and rhythm, during the pranayama exercise described in the fourth rule. In this way, the affirmations will qualify and condition the life of the etheric body, leading eventually to changes in the outer life of the personality.[31]

Rule Seven

> Let the disciple turn his attention to the enunciating of those sounds which echo in the halls where walks the Master. Let him not sound the lesser notes which awaken vibration within the halls of Maya.[32]

In addition to the four kingdoms of nature discussed in chapter 1, there is also a fifth, or spiritual, kingdom. Members of this fifth kingdom are sometimes called Masters of the Wisdom. These Masters were once members of the fourth, or human, kingdom. By applying the processes of character building and meditation, they learned the needed lessons in the human school, stepped off the great Wheel of Rebirth (discussed in chapter 1), and became members of the higher kingdom. In theosophical terminology, a Master of the Wisdom has taken the fifth spiritual initiation.

The seventh rule distinguishes between inspiration and mediumship. *Inspiration* is the main technique used by the Masters of the Wisdom when working with human beings in the physical world.[33] It is a transmission of understanding that occurs from soul to soul, implying that it occurs via the abstract levels of the mental plane. In this rule, "the halls where walks the Master" refers to those abstract levels. Inspiration presupposes a relatively high point in evolution for both the transmitter and the recipient. The recipient experiences inspiration via the crown chakra and does not utilize a psychic ability. After gaining an abstract or nonverbal understanding of some idea, the recipient may then employ both mind and brain to express that idea in his or her own thoughts and images.[34]

On the other hand, *mediumship* is a transfer of information from the various levels of the emotional, or astral, plane. Because the astral is the plane of glamour and of a distorted presentation of reality, the astral levels are called "the halls of Maya" in this rule. Mediumship is experienced via the solar plexus chakra and utilizes a psychic ability. The three most common psychic abilities are clairaudience, psychometry, and clairvoyance. *Clairaudience* is the ability to hear or perceive sounds from the astral plane. *Psychometry* is the ability to divine knowledge about an object or about a person connected with it through contact with the object. *Clairvoyance* is the ability to perceive images from the astral plane. Through using one or more of these psychic abilities, a person can be a medium without having any mental or spiritual evolution. A trance medium receives information while in a hypnotic trance, and neither mind nor soul is involved in the process.

Now let us consider the meaning of the seventh rule. Turn your attention to preparing yourself for experiencing inspiration ("let the disciple turn his attention"). This preparation requires three efforts. By applying the fifth rule, develop the faculty of abstract thought and the power of linking with your soul. By applying the sixth rule, correct the faults in your behavior. And by cultivating the ability to serve, demonstrate that you have something to give. Through right meditation, self-correction, and service, the vibration of your consciousness can reach the abstract levels of the mental plane and attract the attention of the Masters of the Wisdom who reside there ("to the enunciating of those sounds which echo in the halls where walks the Master"). When you are sufficiently prepared, your meditation can be augmented and enhanced by receiving inspiration from a Master.[35]

On the other hand, you should avoid psychic development exercises that lead to communication with the astral plane ("let him not sound the lesser notes which awaken vibration within the halls of Maya"). These exercises are generally a combination of a breathing technique, special posture, self-hypnosis, and visualization. Avoid those exercises because otherwise you may be deceived by the phenomena of the astral plane. Individual, national, and racial desires are constantly constructing forms out of astral matter, which then appear as an illusory panorama. The astral forms can be contacted through mediumship and then be interpreted as conveying guidance. Since these forms can masquerade as famous beings, such as Jesus or Buddha, you may be completely deceived by them. Discarnate entities also pass through the astral plane, either out of or toward incarnation, and can be contacted through mediumship. Because these entities range in character from the very good to the very bad, you may also be completely deceived by them. Frequently, the contacted entities are not highly evolved and are quite incapable of employing the inspiration method of communication. Undesirable forces and entities do exist; therefore, it is a mistake to give blind and unquestioning acceptance to any form of guidance.[36]

By applying the rules of character building and meditation for the path of probation, aspirants are able to take the first initiation and begin traveling on the path of discipleship. On this new path, they are sometimes called "accepted disciples" because each one has been accepted by some Master. They work with their Masters in two different ways: at night, when they are asleep and out of their physical bodies, and through inspiration during meditation periods for which they have provided the right conditions. However, the method of inspiration occurs infrequently during the early stages because new disciples seldom provide the right conditions.[37]

Chapter 3

Advanced Rules for Character Building

The first initiation corresponds to the dissipation of the etheric web separating the solar plexus chakra from the heart chakra, enabling the kundalini energy to reach and stimulate the heart chakra. It is an expansion of consciousness, resulting in the realization of an increased unity with all that lives. It brings about an increased unification of the personality with the soul, and it is similar to a school experience in which you suddenly realize that you have mastered a lesson and are ready to pass into a higher grade. Finally, the first initiation is the moment when a person leaves the path of probation and starts on the path of discipleship.

This chapter interprets the last seven of Bailey's rules as describing a sevenfold process of character building for the path of discipleship. These rules fall into two divisions. Rules Eight through Ten give instruction for the period between the first and second initiations, and rules Eleven through Fourteen give instruction for the period between the second and third initiations.

Rule Eight

> When the disciple nears the portal, the Greater Seven
> must awaken and bring forth response from the lesser
> seven upon the double circle.[1]

Because this rule refers to the endocrine glands, it may be
helpful to review some information about them. A gland is
defined to be *endocrine* if it produces a hormone that is secreted
in the blood and if this hormone exerts a specific effect on some
organ or process at a distance from the gland. The study of
endocrinology has revealed that certain results arise from activity in the glands, and medication has been developed to stimulate or retard the activity of a given gland. Certain types of
people illustrate glandular activity or passivity, but it is impos-
sible to make fundamental changes in people by treating only
their glands. The endocrine glands, although potent, are only
the effects of certain inner causes.[2]

As discussed in the chapter 1, the physical body has two
divisions: the dense physical body and the etheric body. The
etheric body is sometimes called the "etheric double" because
each organ in the dense physical body has a counterpart, or a
double, in the etheric body. In particular, each endocrine
gland is associated with a specific etheric chakra; Table 1 in
chapter 1 gives those associations. The gland can be viewed as
being the dense counterpart, creation, or precipitation of the
corresponding chakra, and it responds to the awakened or
unawakened condition of that chakra.

In the first rule of chapter 1, the word "door" was used at
the beginning of the path of probation to symbolize the objective for that path—namely, the first initiation. Now, in the
eighth rule, this symbol reappears as the word "portal" and
represents the objective for the path of discipleship—namely,
the third initiation. The other symbols in the eighth rule have
the following meanings: "Greater Seven" refers to the seven

etheric chakras; "lesser seven," to the associated seven endo-crine glands; and "double circle," to the dense physical body.

The first phrase in the eighth rule is "when the disciple nears the portal." At the beginning of the path of discipleship, disciples are able to express virtuous behavior, which resolves the cleavage sensed at the beginning of the path of probation. However, they become aware of a new sense of cleavage: the discrepancy between the consciousness and attitude of the soul on one side and the thoughts and motives of the personality on the other side. Integrating the new cleavage is equivalent to attaining the third initiation. Disciples grasp the significant fact that achieving this integration is the portal that would enable them to enter higher realms of being and to wield additional powers. Thus, they are motivated to begin a new cycle in the process of character building, and their initial effort is continuing the application of the *as if* technique described in the seventh rule (chapter 1). When they make additional progress and come nearer to the third initiation, they come nearer to *knowing* themselves as they truly are. As a result, they improve the ability of the personality to contact the energies of the soul—namely, the energies of will, love, and wisdom.[3]

The second phrase is "the Greater Seven must awaken." After increasing their sensitivity to higher energies, disciples must make another effort: learning how to sweep those energies through the mental, emotional, and etheric bodies, thereby expelling that which hinders and perfecting an instrument through which the soul can function and be apparent. Thus, they need to enter a prolonged period of observation, discover the various energies that they contact, and then experiment with directing those energies. Through this process, disciples can become scientific workers in the field of hidden energies and discover the reality of the seven chakras in the etheric body. These force centers are the medium through which any energy from a higher dimension must pass, no matter from what source, before that energy can make an impact on the physical brain or be outwardly displayed. Disciples can eventually reach the point when they know what they are doing, know with what energies they are working, and can call their etheric chakras into intelligent cooperation with their purposes and ideas. By first contacting the energies of the soul and then directing those energies, as learned through trial and error, each disciple can ensure that the seven major chakras awaken with the energies of the soul.[4]

The third phrase is "bring forth response from the lesser seven upon the double circle." The endocrine glands keep the bloodstream supplied with hormones that are essential to physical health, and they produce the necessary resistance to infections. The endocrine glands also condition and influence physical behavior — for example, by affecting how daily events are interpreted and determining the passivity or activity of reactions to those events. Because the quality and livingness of the etheric chakras control the endocrine glands, the awakening of the chakras with energies from the soul must bring forth an automatic response from the seven glands in the dense physical body. This response will produce greater physiological balance and more sensitive activity on the physical plane.[5]

As discussed in chapter 1, the path of probation is concerned with several physical disciplines, such as vegetarianism, fasting, adhering to theories of virtuous behavior, and possibly celibacy. These disciplines help aspirants to improve their health and to gain control over their physical appetites and lower nature. However, the path of discipleship is not based on physical disciplines, and disciples should no longer emphasize them. Instead, what is important is learning how to contact the energies of the soul and how to direct those energies through the mental, emotional, and etheric bodies. The automatic response of the endocrine glands will then improve both health and outer behavior, but those dense physical reactions are the effects rather than the goal of the new effort.[6]

Rule Nine

Let the disciple merge himself within the circle of his
other selves. Let but one colour blend them and their
unity appear. Only when the group is known and
sensed can energy be wisely emanated.[7]

Travelers on the spiritual path need to recognize certain
major frameworks of development. After learning to master
what lies within one particular framework, they find that it is
only a small portion of a still greater whole, within which they
must also learn to function. On the path of probation, aspirants
work within the individual framework of the blending personality and soul, and their principal lesson is learning to express
inclusive love through outer behavior. According to the eighth
rule, disciples begin the path of discipleship by also working
within the individual framework. They will continue to work
within that framework during the remainder of the path of
discipleship and then later during the path of initiation.[8]

After achieving a certain measure of success with the
eighth rule, disciples are ready to add a new dimension by
working within the larger framework of a group. Because their
next principal lesson is learning to express inclusive love
through the emotional body, they begin to realize that the
group framework helps to teach them what they must learn and
that it is also their destined field of service. Aspirants may have
been part of a group on the path of probation, but that group
was gathered around a particular teacher, guru, or therapist
who acted as an external authority and focal point. However,
in the group framework described here, there is no individual
leader. Instead, each member seeks to be guided by the light of
the soul, which means by one's own inner understanding.

How can an appropriate group be formed? By applying
the eighth rule, disciples learn to stand in greater firmness in
spiritual being and work more consciously with their soul
aspect. Then, and only then, will their souls call to them those
who can be their true collaborators. They should not look for

collaborators among those whom they help, who have gathered around them, or who have acquiesced to their teachings because such people have not yet found sufficient self-confidence and innate strength. Nor should they look among people who are sweet, gentle, and kind but also ineffectual. Instead, they should look for people who do not need their help but seek their collaboration, who respond with love to the need of humanity and are effective in their activity, and who can use their minds to distinguish between visionary dreams that may materialize in the far distant future and those ideals whose time has come to be manifested on earth.[9]

The ninth rule describes three stages of group work on the path of discipleship. The symbols are defined as follows: "circle" refers to the external group; "other selves," to the collaborators; "one colour," to the single purpose of serving humanity; and "group," to the associated inner group within the spiritual kingdom of nature.

In the first stage of group work, disciples should merge themselves within the group of other collaborators ("let the disciple merge himself within the circle of his other selves"). In particular, they should learn to subordinate their own ideas of personal growth to the group requirements; eliminate their glamours because the feelings, reactions, and wishes of the individual do not count; carefully watch their thoughts about the others, eliminating all suspicion and criticism; and hold the others in the pure light of love, helping to release their bonds and lift the entire group. Through melding and unifying the group, each member can work in close mental rapport and spiritual cooperation with the others.[10]

In the second stage, the members of the group should unitedly strive to be motivated by the single purpose of serving humanity ("let but one colour blend them"), enabling their selfish motives to die from attrition and lack of attention. When the group succeeds in fusing itself with this purpose, it becomes united with the fifth, or spiritual, kingdom of nature, and the unity appears in the form of group inspiration ("and their unity appear"). Because the group may consist of members at different points of evolution, group inspiration does not imply that all members directly receive inspiration. Only the senior members, those with a sufficiently advanced status, receive the outline of the divine plan from the spiritual kingdom. After this outline has been received, other members may help to devise and coordinate the implementation of the plan, giving proper attention to the general picture and to the details of immediate needs. In any case, each member of the group should enlist his or her free will and intelligent understanding during this stage to give full intellectual and intuitive assent to the projects that emerge.[11]

In the third stage, the group works as a channel for the distribution of certain types of forces in the physical world. When this stage is reached, the group has some distinguishing characteristic and is dedicated to some specific form of service. According to Bailey, there are nine different types of groups, plus a synthesizing tenth group consisting of representatives from the other nine. These ten types of groups are listed and described in Table 2 on pages 50–51. Each of these types has an inner counterpart within the spiritual kingdom. An outer group may be only partial and fragmentary, but the inner counterpart is a completed whole. Each outer group attempts to manifest a specific type of energy that is embodied by its associated inner counterpart. Only when inspiration from the inner group is known and sensed ("only when the group is known and sensed") can energy be wisely emanated from the outer group ("can energy be wisely emanated"). Depending on the outer group, the emanating energy may be in the form of vital healing forces, scientific discoveries, advancements in psychotherapy, or new ideas in politics, economics, or religion.[12]

In the preceding paragraph, the inner groups play a role similar to that of the Muses in Greek mythology. The Muses were divinities in heaven, or goddesses of Olympus, who brought inspiration to human beings. They were a band of nine sisters and were the daughters of Zeus, who was the

Table 2. Types of Bridging Groups

Number	Name	Description
1	Telepathic communicators	"These people are receptive to impression from the Masters and from each other; they are the custodians of group purpose and, therefore, closely related to all the other types of groups."
2	Trained observers	"Their objective is to see clearly through all events, through space and time by means of the cultivation and use of the intuition."
3	Magnetic healers	"They work intelligently with the vital force of the etheric body. The work to be done is that of the intelligent transmission of energy to various parts of the nature—mental, emotional and physical."
4	Educators of the New Age	"Their service is along the line of culture and they will work to bring in the new type of education. Their emphasis will be upon the building of the antahkarana and upon the use of the mind in meditation."
5	Political organizers	"They will work in the world of human government, dealing with the problems of civilisation and with the relationships existing between nations. The bringing about of international understanding will be their major objective."
6	Workers in the field of religion	"Their work is to formulate the universal platform of the new world religion. It is a work of loving synthesis and it will emphasize the unity and the fellowship of the spirit."

supreme ruler of the gods, and Mnemosyne, which means "Memory." In the earliest myths, the Muses were not distinguished from each other; but in later ones, each had her own special field, such as history, astronomy, dance, and lyric poetry.

To understand the remaining rules in this chapter, it is important to remember that disciples need to work within both group and individual frameworks. The three stages of group

Table 2. Continued

Number	Name	Description
7	Scientific servers	"They will reveal the essential spirituality of all scientific work which is motivated by love of humanity and its welfare, which relates science and religion and brings to light the glory of God through the medium of His tangible world and His works."
8	Psychologists	"Their major task will be to relate, through approved techniques, the soul and the personality, leading to the revelation of divinity through the medium of humanity. They will act also as transmitters of illumination between groups of thinkers and as illuminators of group thought."
9	Financiers and economists	"They will work with the energies and forces which express themselves through the interchange and the values of commerce; they will deal with Law of Supply and Demand and with the great principle of *Sharing* which ever governs divine purpose."
10	Creative workers	"They link and blend life and form creatively. Their work is also largely philosophical and concerned with the task of relating—factually and scientifically—the other nine types of groups so that they may work creatively upon the physical plane and the divine Plan may clearly appear as a result of this synthesis which they bring about."

Source: A. A. Bailey, *Discipleship in the New Age,* vol. 1 (1944; reprint; New York: Lucis Publishing Company, 1976), 35–40.

work can be summarized as group unity, group meditation, and group activity, and they are meant to span the rest of the path of discipleship. On the other hand, the remaining rules give instruction for the individual framework for the rest of that path. The group framework can be thought of as being the context that underlies, motivates, and supports those remaining rules.

Rule Ten

The Army of the Voice, the devas in their serried
ranks, work ceaselessly. Let the disciple apply himself
to the consideration of their methods; let him learn
the rules whereby that Army works within the veils of
Maya.[13]

The third rule in chapter 1 instructed aspirants to purify
their emotions by using a process of substitution: removing
attention from self-centered feelings, calling in the higher
rhythms of the soul, and then allowing the new rhythms to
supersede those of the personality. To participate satisfactorily
in group work, disciples must discover the need for further
purifying their emotional lives and become ready to learn a
more advanced technique.

Before discussing that new technique, let us consider the
meaning of the word *devas*, which appears in the tenth rule.
This Sanskrit word means "celestial beings," of which there are
several classes. Devas of one class form the substance of the
physical plane or world; devas of another class form the substance of the emotional plane; and devas of a third class form
the substance of the mental plane. From this point of view, all
physical, emotional, and mental forms are living matter, fabri-
cated by the devas out of the substance of their own bodies.

It may be helpful to contrast human beings with devas.
Human beings are self-conscious; devas are not. Human
beings unfold their inner vision and learn to understand; devas
unfold their inner hearing and learn to follow. Human beings
aim at self-control; devas develop by being controlled. Human
beings have the responsibility to choose what they create. The
devas, who are the sum total of the energy of substance itself,
do not care what forms they build; their task is simply to
respond, with constructive vibration, to the words and sounds
that are directing and controlling them.[14]

In the tenth rule, "the Army" refers to the emotional body;
"Voice," to environmental stimuli and mental thoughts; "devas,"

to the substance underlying emotional reactions and feelings; "rules," to the technique of emotional purification; and "veils of Maya," to the glamours of the astral plane.

The emotional body ("the Army") responds to both outer and inner voices ("of the Voice"). The substance of the emotional body ("the devas in their serried ranks") reacts continually to stimuli from the environment and thoughts from the mind ("work ceaselessly"). Through inquiry into their emotional nature, disciples should apply themselves to discover the relationship between their emotional reactions and those two factors ("let the disciple apply himself to the consideration of their methods"). In particular, they need to discover the technique of purifying emotional reactions through understanding the cause and meaning of those reactions. After they learn to apply that technique, their emotional nature can function without being affected by the glamours of the astral plane ("let him learn the rules whereby that Army works within the veils of Maya").

The tenth rule does not describe the technique of emotional purification but instead describes how we can discover that technique for ourselves. This pedagogical approach is used because we must develop our own understanding to make further progress. If we tried to purify our emotions by following instructions given by someone else, we would not have the self-knowledge needed to be successful. Although a teacher can give appropriate hints or point in a particular direction, we must have the courage and self-reliance to find our own way. Only what we consciously know and experience is of importance, and it constitutes the truth for us.

Through inquiry in the direction pointed by the tenth rule, we can gain a nonverbal understanding of our emotional nature, including how to purify that nature. Here are some things we might learn. The emotional body is a machine that reacts to outer conditions according to its inner programming. A glamour is an emotional reaction, such as pride, self-pity, or criticism, that distorts perception. By changing the inner programming, it is possible to become free of any particular glamour without requiring that any changes be made in the external world. However, becoming free of a glamour is difficult because it involves the loss of some false pride. The necessary approach involves using the mind to examine a specific glamour while at the same time observing the mind. Through this process, the mind's examination can be guided by the soul's wisdom, and any mental resistance and defensiveness regarding the glamour can be observed and eliminated. Through careful scrutiny of the glamour, it is possible to discover the underlying inner programming: specific thoughts and beliefs that involve being identified with objects of desire, with the form aspect, and with what is material. By the determined facing of facts and stern recognition of truth, inner programming can be changed, leading to the disappearance of the glamour.[15]

Rule Eleven

Let the disciple transfer the fire from the lower triangle to the higher, and preserve that which is created through the fire of the midway point.[16]

Character building is concerned with eliminating three types of impurities: maya on the etheric level, glamour on the emotional level, and illusion on the mental level. As shown in chapter 1, aspirants work on eliminating all three types of impurities. However, they must primarily demonstrate physical control to attain the first initiation, which means overcoming maya and displaying virtuous behavior. As shown by rules Eight through Ten in this chapter, disciples work on eliminating all three types of impurities during the period between the first and second initiations. But they must primarily demonstrate emotional control to attain the second initiation, which means dissipating glamour through understanding its cause and meaning. The remaining rules, Eleven through Fourteen, give instruction for the path of discipleship between the second and third initiations. Although disciples still work on eliminating all three types of impurities during this final period, they must primarily demonstrate mental control to attain the third initiation. Mental control requires that the soul itself take the dominant position and dispel illusion.

Both upward and downward trends of energy are present within the etheric body. Rule Eleven refers to both trends, and the symbols have the following interpretations: "the fire" refers to the energies of the three lower chakras; "lower triangle," to the solar plexus, sacral, and basic chakras; "higher," to the higher triangle consisting of the head center (formed by the crown and brow chakras), throat chakra, and heart chakra; and "midway point," to the middle or heart chakra.

The first phrase of the rule refers to the upward trend of energy. As part of character building, you should learn to transmute your base or lower qualities into higher qualities, which has the effect of transferring the energies of your lower three chakras into the higher ones ("let the disciple transfer the fire from the lower triangle to the higher"). By transmuting sexual or physical creativity into artistic or mental creativity, transfer the energy of the sacral chakra to the throat chakra. By transmuting emotional consciousness into group consciousness, transfer the energy of the solar plexus chakra to the heart chakra. By transmuting material ambition into a dedication to serve humanity, transfer the kundalini energy of the basic chakra to the brow and crown chakras.[17]

The processes of transference take place over a long period. Each of the earlier rules helped to further one or another of them, which in turn helped to awaken and bring into creative activity the associated higher chakra. As discussed in chapter 1, the transfer of energy into the throat chakra began before the path of probation, and the transfer of energy into the heart chakra began during the path of probation. As discussed in chapter 2, the etheric webs in the spine impede the move-

ment of the kundalini energy, implying that the transfer of this
energy must occur in ordered stages. You are able to complete
the transfer of kundalini into the head center when you have
taken the second initiation, corresponding to the dissipation of
the last web that can block the rising of the kundalini energy,
and when you are contemplating some world problem with the
intent of discovering the meaning of that problem.

Each phrase in each rule has a *training* aspect. For the first
phrase in this rule, the training is going beyond an outer problem and penetrating to the meaning that lies behind it. Events,
circumstances, happenings, and physical phenomena of every
kind are only symbols of what is occurring in the inner worlds,
and you need to penetrate those worlds as far as your perception permits. Start by endeavoring to discover the reason *why*,
and then wrestle with outer happenings to arrive at the meaning they should hold for you. By reasoning from cause to effect
and knowing the reason that certain actions are bound inevita-
bly to produce certain effects, you are able to view human
happenings in terms of deeper universal and spiritual principles. After ascertaining the meaning of any specific event, use
it as an invitation to penetrate more deeply into the newly
revealed world of meaning. Eventually, you can discover that
the world of meaning is spread like an intricate network over all
activities and every aspect of the phenomenal world.[18]

Through penetrating to the meaning of a problem that has
been distressing humanity, you gain an abstract vision of how
that problem can be solved in a fundamental rather than a
superficial way. This type of vision occurs when energy from
the soul pours into the crown chakra. Your next step is to begin
the work of directing, energizing, and coordinating the lower
chakras. The second phrase of the eleventh rule refers to this
downward trend of energy and indicates that there are two
stages.

The first stage is creating a concrete plan or proposal
based on the abstract vision ("that which is created"), which
requires that the crown, throat, and sacral chakras be brought

together in simultaneous and conscious relationship. By bringing about the right relationship between these three chakras, you become creative in a worldly sense and therefore of use to others. However, no plan for a better world can be implemented by only one person. The second stage is preserving and sustaining that plan by establishing right human, group, and spiritual relationships. This is accomplished by employing the inclusive love of the heart chakra ("through the fire of the midway point"), requiring that the crown, heart, and solar plexus chakras be brought together in simultaneous and close cooperation. As a result, selfish individual love is transformed into group love, enabling personal motivations to be transformed into impersonal ones. The first stage of the downward trend has a paramount effect on the mental body, and the second stage primarily affects the emotional body.[19]

Rule Twelve

Let the disciple learn the use of the hand in service;
let him seek the mark of the messenger in his feet,
and let him learn to see with the eye that looks out
from between the two.[20]

After making progress with the preceding rule, disciples are ready to learn three different ways of expressing soul consciousness in the physical world: rendering practical service, working as outer messengers for the Masters of the Wisdom, and using the third eye, referring to the synthesis of the crown and brow chakras. Each of these ways is described by a phrase in the twelfth rule.

The first phrase refers to service. As indicated by the fourth rule in the chapter 1, aspirants begin the process of serving on the path of probation. While on that path, their service generally is characterized by a combination of good intentions, mixed motives, and fanaticism. In contrast, true service is guided by wisdom, motivated by inclusive love, and provided without attachment. After attaining the second initiation, disciples have the capacity of rendering true service, for which the preceding rule gave instruction for the preliminary steps: contemplating some world problem until an abstract vision of a solution is received, converting this vision into concrete plans and proposals, and then establishing right human, group, and spiritual relationships. The final step is learning the use of the hands for materializing those plans and proposals ("let the disciple learn the use of the hand"), enabling service to be rendered in a practical way in the physical world ("in service"). This step is needed because the hands are the physical body's primary organs for manipulating physical materials, such as typewriters, automobiles, food, and clothing.

The second phrase refers to an unusual relationship that each disciple can have with the spiritual kingdom of nature, comprising the Masters of the Wisdom. After meeting certain requirements, the disciple can be granted the privilege of being able to call the attention of a particular Master during an emergency and then being *guaranteed* a response. When granted this privilege, the disciple is technically called a Chela on the Thread, the thread being formed out of energy that the Master projects to the disciple. Along this thread, the disciple sounds a call and receives a response in the form of strength, knowledge, and advice from the Master. The concept of the Chela on the Thread lies behind the distorted teaching regarding the prerogatives and privileges of the priesthood, such as in the relation of the pope to God or in the symbols associated with the Brahmin caste in India.[21]

A Chela on the Thread is an outer messenger for the inner spiritual kingdom, and disciples should seek the status of being such messengers ("let him seek the mark of the messenger"). An outer messenger does the difficult work of materializing the needed forms in the physical world and making the necessary human contacts, such as through traveling ("in his feet"). To prepare themselves for this privilege, disciples need to meet the following requirements: establishing and prolonging the contemplative state of mind, as indicated by the eleventh rule; rendering practical service, as indicated by the first portion of the present rule; and having the capacity to handle their personal lives and individual problems by themselves so that they can be trusted to call on the spiritual kingdom only for purposes of group service.[22]

Because of the ability to communicate with a discarnate being, it may seem that a Chela on the Thread is necessarily psychic. However, the mode of communication is different from that used by the average psychic in several important respects. Due to the presence of the thread, the disciple can have frequent, conscious, and deliberate contacts with one particular Master and yet be unable to register any impression coming from the astral plane. In contrast, a person with a typical psychic ability, such as clairaudience or clairvoyance, can receive impressions coming from the many different forces, entities, and thoughtforms residing on the astral plane. A Chela on the Thread is fully conscious and in control of his or her experience, whereas a psychic is often in a trance and out of control. A Chela on the Thread always works through the crown chakra, whereas the average psychic works through the solar plexus chakra. Being a Chela on the Thread is a privilege that has been granted, whereas a psychic ability is an innate capacity that has been developed. For the above reasons, being a Chela on the Thread is independent of what is usually regarded as psychic unfoldment.

The third phrase of the rule refers to the third eye, sometimes called the eye of the Magician. This inner eye is formed by the synthesis, or vibratory interaction, between the forces of the personality working through the brow chakra and the forces of the soul working through the crown chakra. Through application of the eleventh rule, the kundalini energy is raised into the brow chakra and then into the crown chakra, whereas energy from soul levels pours into the crown chakra first and then into the brow chakra. When these personality and soul forces interact and are potent enough, the third eye comes into being in the etheric body. This process can be thought of as reenacting the drama of sexual procreation on a higher level: mother-personality and father-soul unite and are at-one, and then the third eye is born. According to the Bible, "Except a man be born again, he cannot see the kingdom of God" (John 3:3). The formation of the third eye is the second birth, bringing a power of vision that enables the personality to express itself as the soul on the physical plane.[23]

Each disciple should learn to see with the third eye, which takes the semblance of an eye looking out between the two dense physical eyes ("let him learn to see with the eye that looks out from between the two"). The third eye has three main functions. First, it enables the personality to perceive with the vision of the soul. The dense physical eye can register physical form, but the third eye can see behind any physical form and contact the underlying soul. This vision dispels illusion and illumines the mind. Second, it is the controlling factor in white-magical work. When alignment is right and attitude correct, the will aspect of the soul can function through the focused third eye and produce constructive results in the material world. As an analogy, the dense physical eye has the often-noticed power to control other human beings and animals by a look or through steady gazing. Just as force flows through the focused dense physical eye, force also flows through the focused third eye. Third, it is the agent of the soul in purificatory work with the personality. The power of the third eye can have a disintegrating and destroying effect, eliminating wrong identifications, breaking down habit patterns that cause inefficiency, and driving out other remaining forms of maya. Through this process, uncoordinated living can be transmuted into integrated activity, enabling one to employ only those forces and energies that serve and fulfill one's intent.[24]

Rule Thirteen

Four things the disciple must learn and comprehend before he can be shewn that inmost mystery: first, the laws of that which radiates; the five meanings of magnetization make the second; the third is transmutation, or the secret lost of alchemy; and lastly the first letter of the Word which has been imparted, or the hidden name egoic.[25]

By applying the first portion of the twelfth rule, disciples were able to perform practical service by materializing their abstract visions in the physical world. At that stage, however, they may not have been in touch with the divine plan because their abstract visions may have come from the wisdom aspect of the soul rather than from a higher level. Also, they may not have been working in an effective, coordinated, and integrated way. By applying the second portion of the twelfth rule, disciples became Chelas on the Thread, enabling them to be outer messengers for the custodians of the divine plan. And by applying the third portion, they learned to use the power of the third eye for integrating their personalities. According to the thirteenth rule, they are able to increase the value and significance of their service by bringing these three factors together.

Before discussing the meaning of the thirteenth rule as a whole, it may be helpful to consider the meaning of the individual symbols, which are listed in four different phrases. The first phrase is "the laws of that which radiates." It is important to notice that these words do not refer to the laws of radiation but to the laws of *that which radiates*. The soul is the factor in a human being that makes its presence felt as light or luminous radiation. The soul is the "self-shining from within," and a human being can truly radiate only when the soul aspect is dominant. Thus, the first phrase actually refers to the laws of the soul. These laws concern the life of the soul on its own plane and the relationship that the blending soul and personality learn to establish with other souls and with the spiritual kingdom of nature.[26]

The second phrase is "the five meanings of magnetization." Whereas love attracts, the mind can attract, repel, and coordinate. This phrase refers to the mind's power of attracting or magnetizing information because the mind can attract information from five different levels: intuitive ideas from the spiritual dimension of life, wisdom from the soul, facts and data from the concrete memory, feelings from the emotional body, and perceptions from the physical senses.[27]

The third phrase is "transmutation, or the secret lost of alchemy." The word *transmutation* refers to transforming a lower quality into a higher one. Five different types of transmutation can be accomplished through character building. As indicated by the fourth rule in chapter 1, sexual or physical creativity can be transmuted into artistic or mental creativity, and emotional consciousness can be transmuted into group consciousness. As indicated by the eleventh rule, material ambition can be transmuted into a dedication to serve humanity, and the twelfth rule indicates uncoordinated living can be transmuted into integrated activity. In the present rule, personality activity can be transmuted into spiritual living. However, this tabulation constitutes a wide generalization; the transmutation process is not necessarily carried forward in any sequential fashion or as smoothly as the above order might suggest.[28]

The fourth phrase is "the first letter of the Word which has been imparted, or the hidden name egoic." The typology of the seven rays is a classification of basic qualities of energy and is applicable to many different forms of energy. Table 3 lists the name, quality, and basic technique for each of the seven rays. The first three rays are the major rays; the last four are the minor ones. The fourth phrase refers to the application of this typology to soul energy. The hidden nature, or name, of each human being is that person's soul energy, and this nature consists of seven different qualities, or letters, corresponding to the seven rays. As discussed in chapter 1, the soul consists of three primary qualities — namely, will, love, and wisdom — corresponding to the three major rays. These qualities of the soul are created by the response of the mental plane to the impact of energy imparted from the spiritual triad. The mutual interplay of these three primary qualities then produces the four minor qualities, or rays. As an analogy, the visible spectrum consists of seven different colors; three of these colors are primary and can be combined to produce the other four colors.[29]

Next let us consider the meaning of the thirteenth rule as a whole. There are four aspects of service that disciples must learn and comprehend ("four things the disciple must learn and comprehend") before they can display the methods and techniques of the new emerging civilization ("before he can be shewn that inmost mystery"). This emerging civilization is actually the spiritual kingdom of nature; it already exists on the inner planes and is slowly becoming externalized on the physical plane.

First, disciples need to know the following laws of the soul ("the laws of that which radiates"). Inspiration is received via the soul. As discussed in chapter 2, an individual can receive inspiration by establishing three conditions: right meditation, self-correction, and service. In the past, the consciousness of humanity was raised through the inspiration of its foremost individuals. But in the future, the consciousness of humanity will be raised through the inspiration of certain groups. This change will occur because enough people with the necessary sensitivity will be available to form groups and because the newer truths of the coming era can be grasped only as a result of group endeavor. However, group inspiration requires conditions beyond those needed for individual inspiration. According to the ninth rule in this chapter, the group as a whole must pass through the stages of group unity and group meditation.[30]

Second, disciples must know how to use their minds for magnetizing information from five different levels ("the five meanings of magnetization"). In particular, they use their

Table 3. The Seven Rays

Ray	Name	Quality	Technique
One	Will or power	Dynamic purpose	Grasping
Two	Love-wisdom	Love	Attracting
Three	Active intelligence	Intellect	Selecting
Four	Harmony through conflict	Unification	At-one-ing
Five	Concrete knowledge or science	Discrimination	Differentiating
Six	Devotion or idealism	Sensitivity	Responding
Seven	Ceremonial order or magic	Appearance	Coordinating

Source: A. A. Bailey, *Esoteric Psychology*, vol. 2 (1942; reprint; New York: Lucis Publishing Company, 1975), 83.

minds for receiving inspiration from the spiritual kingdom outlining the immediate aspect of the divine plan. Next, to work out their contributions to that evolutionary process, they use their minds for receiving and combining three types of information: wisdom from their souls, knowledge from their concrete memories, and perceptions from their physical senses regarding opportunities present in the physical world. Finally, before beginning to implement their contributions, they pause and use their minds for observing their emotional responses.

Third, disciples must know the meaning of "transmutation, or the secret lost of alchemy." During the Middle Ages, alchemy was concerned with how one state of being is transmuted into another state through the agency of fire. In the case considered here, disciples need to know how personality activity is transmuted into spiritual living through the downflow of inspiration and wisdom. However, this transmutation can occur only if the emotional body has the right condition. Thus, a key preliminary step is dissipating any observed glamour by using the technique referred to in the tenth rule. If disciples can avoid glamour, then the downflow of inspiration and wisdom will automatically flood their personality lives with effective unselfish love and with devotion to the divine plan, devotion to those whom the plan serves, and devotion to those who serve the plan. They will have no room for self-interest, self-assertiveness, or self-centered ambition but will consider only the world need and the driving necessity to take the next immediate step for meeting that need.[31]

Fourth, disciples must know how to use the first ray of their soul energy ("the first letter of the Word"). According to Table 3, the first ray is the quality of will or power, and it is the result of higher energy that has been imparted from the spiritual triad ("which has been imparted"). By focusing the will quality, the third eye can galvanize the lower five chakras into activity and bring them under rhythmic control. Then, automatically, the dense physical body will respond in a coordinated and integrated way, revealing outwardly the hidden nature of the soul ("the hidden name egoic").

Rule Fourteen

Listen, touch, see, apply, know.[32]

In this book, two different rules give instruction regarding psychic unfoldment. According to the seventh rule in chapter 2, such experiences are definitely undesirable for aspirants on the path of probation. However, the present rule indicates that psychic sensitivity can be appropriate on the path of discipleship.

People with psychic abilities often have smug self-satisfaction and closed minds, thinking that their abilities indicate an advanced type of spiritual unfoldment. However, they forget that the aboriginal races and animals are all psychic and register what the more mental types fail to record. They also forget that psychism has been part of the religious activities of primitive people since antiquity. For instance, psychic practices can be found today in voodooism or shamanism, and they were part of the indigenous religion in Palestine before the coming of the Israelites, as shown by the admonitions given by Moses to his followers:

> When thou art come into the land which the Lord thy God giveth thee, thou shalt not learn to do after the abominations of those nations. There shalt not be found among you any one that . . . useth divination, or an observer of times, or an enchanter, or a witch, or a charmer, or a consulter with familiar spirits, or a wizard, or a necromancer. For all that do these things are an abomination unto the Lord: and because of these abominations the Lord thy God doth drive them out from before thee (Deut. 18:9–12).

In this quotation, "divination" refers to fortune-telling; "observer of times," to astrology; "enchanter" and "charmer," to hypnotists; and "witch," "consulter with familiar spirits," "wizard," and "necromancer," to various types of psychics.

Why do spiritual teachers such as Moses warn against psychic experiences? Because average psychics are emotionally polarized, they generally misinterpret the meaning of their experiences. Although they may think that they are receiving important information from the inner worlds, they may be just abstracting the contents of their own subconscious minds. Or they may be receiving teachings from discarnate entities who are relatively unevolved. Or they may be unable to differentiate the sensed images and sounds into that which is past, present, and future. Or they may be tuning in on the forebodings of other people while believing that those forebodings refer to their own coming experiences. Furthermore, if they are trance mediums, they have forfeited their free will and are little better than instinctual animals that obsessing entities can occupy and use. Just as the lack of physical control is deemed highly undesirable, lack of psychic control should be considered in the same way. By giving up control, a trance medium is in definite danger of succumbing to various forms of mental illness and may be letting loose forces of a most undesirable character upon the world.[33]

Nevertheless, psychic phenomena are part of the divine expression and are of an essentially higher nature than the purely material processes of living in the physical body. Because disciples cannot put any aspect of manifestation outside their range of experience, they should be prepared for all experiences and face the fact that eventually *all disciples have to become psychics.* How can disciples rescue and safeguard someone who has been deluded by the astral plane if they are afraid to enter the realms of life where psychism rules? How can they be of service in that arena if they have no experience in distinguishing and interpreting different types of phenomena? As a safeguard for themselves, they should rule out all trance conditions and not demonstrate their psychic powers until after their intuitional power is functioning. In this way, their psychic abilities can be controlled and operated from the level of higher consciousness.[34]

Let us now interpret the fourteenth rule. At the stage of the spiritual path represented by this rule, disciples have already unfolded and utilized their intuitional power to receive wisdom, insights, and inspiration. As a result, they have the emotional stability, mental control, and intuitive understanding needed for safely and for wisely using any psychic powers that might arise. Nevertheless, this rule does not encourage disciples to cultivate psychic abilities; it simply asks that they hold themselves in *guarded readiness* to "listen," "touch," and "see" on all levels of service. In particular, they should be prepared to experience clairaudience, psychometry, and clairvoyance, which are the psychic counterparts of physical listening, touching, and seeing. When their psychic abilities do unfold, they should "apply" their intuitional power for interpreting their experiences correctly so that they can "know" exactly what they are hearing, touching, and seeing on the astral plane. By using their psychic abilities with full consciousness, full control, and accurate interpretation, they can extend their range of service to include both the physical and astral worlds.[35]

Chapter 4

Advanced Rules for Meditation

When undergoing training for initiation, the first thing that students need to discover is where they stand on the spiritual path because that knowledge enables them to learn what they should do to make further progress. For instance, one student may have reached the point where the light of the personality should be trained on the soul. Another student may be at a higher point and should turn the light of the soul on the personality, thereby becoming a soul-infused personality. And another student may have reached a still higher point and should direct the light of the spiritual triad on the soul-infused personality. Because a high point in evolution can be reached unconsciously, people are frequently not truly aware of where they are. Although a teacher may give appropriate hints, it is important that each student discover his or her point of evolution through self-inquiry. If someone else tells you about your place on the evolutionary ladder, that information may be wrong, and it may prevent you from developing your own self-knowledge, self-reliance, and inner conviction. After discovering your status, you should rigidly keep that knowledge to yourself. If you do have a position in front of that of the average citizen, that fact will be demonstrated by a life of active service and by the manifestation of an illumined vision.[1]

The rules discussed in this book are in the form of veiled hints of truth. They encompass a vast structure of information and represent many stages and principles. By first being aware of your point of attainment, you can discover the particular rule that clarifies your way, that leads to revelation, and that is in line with your next delineated step.

In this chapter, the last seven of Bailey's rules are interpreted as giving progressive instruction in meditation for the path of discipleship. Rules Eight through Ten give instruction for the period between the first and second initiations. Rules Eleven through Fourteen give instruction for the period between the second and third initiations.

Rule Eight

When the disciple nears the portal, the Greater Seven must awaken and bring forth response from the lesser seven upon the double circle.[2]

Before interpreting this rule, it is necessary to give some technical information regarding the chakras. Each etheric chakra is sometimes symbolized as a lotus consisting of a specific number of petals. For instance, Table 4 lists the numbers of petals in the chakras according to Bailey, which are identical to numbers given earlier by Leadbeater. Traditional Hindu treatises on the chakras also give identical numbers for the lower five chakras but generally depict the brow chakra as having two petals and the crown chakra as having one thousand petals. In this commentary, we will use the petal numbers listed in Table 4. We will consider each petal as representing a particular type of force and interpret the number of petals associated with a

Table 4. Number of Petals in Each Etheric Chakra

Chakra	Number of Petals
Crown	There is an inner circle of 12 major petals surrounded by an outer circle of 960 petals.
Brow	There are 2 primary petals, each of which is further subdivided into 48 smaller petals, so there are 96 petals altogether.
Throat	16 petals
Heart	12 petals
Solar plexus	10 petals
Sacral	6 petals
Basic	4 petals

Sources: A. A. Bailey, *Esoteric Healing* (1953; reprint; New York: Lucis Publishing Company, 1977), 149; A. A. Bailey, *Letters on Occult Meditation* (1922; reprint; New York: Lucis Publishing Company, 1974), 77–78; A. A. Bailey, *A Treatise on White Magic* (1934; reprint; New York: Lucis Publishing Company, 1974), 190, 199.

given chakra as the number of different forces that can be expressed by that chakra.[3]

In the course of evolution, the lower five chakras will be dominated by the brow chakra, and the brow chakra will be dominated by the crown chakra. These relationships can be seen in terms of the petals. The lower five chakras have exactly forty-eight petals. To dominate each petal in the lower five chakras, the brow chakra requires two different forces, or petals, corresponding to the form and quality aspect of the lower petal. Thus, the brow chakra has ninety-sixty petals.

The crown chakra is constructed with two circles of petals. The outer circle has 960 petals, corresponding to 10 petals for each petal in the brow chakra. According to this symbology, each petal in the brow chakra can be dominated by ten different types of intuitions from the crown chakra; the number 10 represents perfection in numerology. For instance, these intuitions can embody the energies of will, love, and wisdom from the soul, insights from the spiritual mind, inspiration from a Master of the Wisdom, and still higher energies from higher planes. Because the inner circle in the crown chakra has twelve

petals, we have the potential ability to comprehend twelve different types of intuitions, which are two more than we can
manifest in the world via the brow chakra. For instance, we
have the potential ability to comprehend the divine purpose
that exists outside of and underlies the manifested world.

The main point of our discussion concerning petals is this:
The two chakras in the head can be thought of as forming seven
different centers of energies. Bailey herself sometimes refers to
the "sevenfold head centre" or to the "seven head centres."[4]
These seven centers of energy are the inner circle of 12 petals
and the outer circle of 960 petals in the crown chakra, plus the
five groups of petals in the brow chakra corresponding to the
lower five chakras.

In the eighth rule, "the portal" refers to the soul; "Greater
Seven," to the seven centers of energy in the head; "lesser
seven," to the seven major etheric chakras; and "double circle,"
to the etheric body, or double.

Let us consider each phrase separately. The first phrase is
"when the disciple nears the portal." At the beginning of the
path of discipleship, you should continue the practice of receptive meditation described in chapter 2. This effort enables you
to receive revelations and guidance regarding your next objective in meditation: transferring your consciousness still higher,
into the wider and inclusive awareness of the soul. When you
make additional progress and come nearer to shifting your
consciousness into the soul, you increase the sensitivity of your
mind to the various types of intuitions that can be received
through the portal of the soul. These intuitions include energies
from both the soul and the spiritual triad, as well as inspiration
from a Master of the Wisdom.

The second phrase is "the Greater Seven must awaken."
The consciousness of the personality operates through the
mind but is centered in the physical brain. To comprehend
fully the intuitions coming from the subtler planes, both your
mind and your brain must correctly register, recognize, and

interpret them. At first, your comprehension of what is sensed or seen on the subtler planes may be slow because it takes time for those contacts to be transmitted via your mind to your brain. This time limitation can be offset by working with rapidity and mental coordination. You also may have difficulty at first in differentiating between the various types of intuitions you are receiving. When transmitting intuitive knowledge via your mind to your brain, learn how to accompany that knowledge with correct recognition and true interpretation. By first making mental contact with various types of intuitions and then working with mental coordination and correct interpretation, you can ensure that the seven centers of energy in your head awaken with intuitive knowledge.[5]

The third phrase is "bring forth response from the lesser seven upon the double circle." Because the seat of the spiritual triad, functioning through the soul, is in the head, all meditation work should be done entirely in the head and from the head. By following the instructions indicated by the first two phrases, you can establish a mutual interplay between the crown and brow chakras. This interplay brings forth a response from the lower five chakras in the etheric double. The point is that *there should be no deliberate meditation work on the chakras*; those centers respond automatically as an effect of meditation. For instance, avoid concentrating on a particular chakra in an effort to awaken that center. Such concentration could result in overstimulation of the nervous system, adversely affect the associated endocrine gland, and open a door to the astral plane that may be difficult to close. Do not work with the lower five chakras, nor aim at their conscious utilization, as clairaudient and clairvoyant persons do. Finally, avoid any practices that deliberately attempt to arouse the kundalini energy and destroy the etheric webs.[6]

Character building and meditation are two different disciplines, though interrelated. The objective of character building is to express the consciousness and attitude of the soul, through the medium of the personality, on the physical plane. As discussed in the preceding chapter, learning to work deliberately with the etheric chakras is appropriate as part of character building. On the other hand, the next objective of meditation is to shift the polarization of consciousness into the soul. Because this effort of shifting occurs on the mental level, any activity occurring on the etheric level is an effect of that effort rather than its goal.

Rule Nine

Let the disciple merge himself within the circle of his other selves. Let but one colour blend them and their unity appear. Only when the group is known and sensed can energy be wisely emanated.[7]

As indicated in the preceding section, receptive meditation is the initial type of meditation practiced on the path of discipleship. This type of meditation is dualistic in nature because the meditator identifies with the personality while being receptive to illumination from the soul. Thus, a *gap in consciousness* remains between the meditator and the soul. When disciples recognize the existence of this gap and realize that receptive meditation cannot bridge it, they become ready to learn another approach.

The Sanskrit word *antahkarana* is a compound word meaning "interior" (*antar*) "sense organ" (*karana*). In theosophy, this word refers to the bridge that is built between the lower, concrete mind, the soul, and the higher, or spiritual, mind. The antahkarana has two segments. The first half extends from the concrete mind to the soul and is gradually built between the first and second initiations. The second half extends from the soul to the spiritual mind and is gradually built between the second and third initiations. The ninth rule gives instructions for building only the first half.

The antahkarana can be thought of as a bridge between the lower world of daily physical living and the higher world of spiritual life. Construction of this bridge requires more than just being oriented to the soul, waiting passively for some activity by the soul to occur. Instead, the construction involves intense mental activity plus the power to imagine and to visualize, and it is primarily an activity of the personality, aided by the soul. Thus, it requires emerging from the realm of devotion into the world of the focused will.[8]

The word *ring-pass-not* is a general term referring to a confining circle or boundary, and this word can apply to many kinds of situations. In the ninth rule, "circle" refers to a mental ring-pass-not that is self-imposed by a meditator. The other symbols in this rule have the following meanings: "other selves" refers to permitted thoughts; "one colour," to an unbroken line of force; and "group," to the unity of the threefold personality and soul.

The ninth rule describes three stages in the process of building the first half of the antahkarana. In the first stage, you should gather your forces into the highest point of your mental consciousness and hold them there within a small ring-pass-not of permitted thoughts ("let the disciple merge himself within the circle of his other selves"). This stage has three steps. The first is the pratyahara exercise given in the second rule in chapter 2; it results in focusing mental energy at the apex of the mind. The second step is to impose upon yourself a mental ring-pass-not that allows only thoughts about the purpose and process of building the antahkarana. The third step is a period of clear thinking while confining your thoughts to within the ring-pass-not. By practicing these steps, you can establish a reservoir of mental energy that previously did not exist, and you can gain a nonverbal understanding regarding the work to be done.[9]

The second stage is visualizing the building process. You must now work slowly, picturing what you want to do, the materials with which you have to work, the stages of your work, and the resultant effects of the planned activity. As part of your visualization, include a picture having an unbroken line of force that blends your emotional body, mental body, and soul ("let but one colour blend them"). While endeavoring to visualize the entire process, you are setting up a definite rapport between the creative imagination of the emotional body, the reservoir of energy in the mental body, and the wisdom aspect of the soul. If the visualization is successful, a current of force actually passes between these three energy centers. Thus, the effort to visualize the unity of these centers allows their unity to appear in actual experience ("and their unity appear").[10]

When you visualize a picture described to you by someone else, you are constructing a rapport, or line of energy, between your emotional body and mind. But here the goal is to construct a line of energy linking the emotional body, mental body, and soul. To achieve that goal through visualization, you need to rely on your own abstract understanding to determine the picture to be visualized. You cannot simply visualize something that you see, read, or remember. Thus, during the first stage of mental activity, it is important to develop the understanding needed for the second stage of visualization.

Although you should construct your picture based on symbols that are meaningful to you, it may be helpful to give one example as an illustration. The personality is represented by a triangle, with the extreme points symbolizing the mental, emotional, and physical bodies. By using an equilateral triangle, the personality is depicted as being coordinated and balanced. Next, a particular color is chosen to represent spiritual aspiration and then is seen as blending with the entire threefold personality. The antahkarana is pictured as a thread of that color extending from the mental body to a radiant body of light representing the soul. Finally, the light of the soul is seen as passing down to the personality, blending with the light of the mind, and then forming one unified light—a searchlight, ready to be turned in any desired direction.

By applying the first and second stages, you can build the first half of the antahkarana. The third stage is consciously using that segment. Only when the unity of the personality and soul is known and sensed through the construction of the antahkarana ("only when the group is known and sensed") can mental energy be wisely used during the third stage ("can energy be wisely emanated"). The first and second stages can be thought of as being a preliminary process of alignment and the third stage as representing additional meditation work that is described in subsequent rules.

Rule Ten

The Army of the Voice, the devas in their serried ranks, work ceaselessly. Let the disciple apply himself to the consideration of their methods; let him learn the rules whereby that Army works within the veils of Maya.[11]

Through applying the preceding rule, meditators increase their awareness of the soul and begin to transmute their consciousness into that of the soul, while still preserving the consciousness of the personality. The soul is the vehicle of abstract thought. By transmuting their consciousness into that of the soul, they are able to sense the abstract meaning of things in two different directions: downward toward the personality and outward toward the rest of the world. According to the tenth rule, disciples should begin with the first direction and learn about the operations of their minds. That learning enables them to work more effectively in the second direction.

The symbols are defined as follows: "the Army" refers to the mental body; "Voice," to sense impressions, emotional reactions, concrete thoughts, wisdom, and insights; "devas," to the substance underlying mental thoughts and activity; "rules," to the stages of mental activity that precede illumination; and "veils of Maya," to the illusions of the mental plane.

The mental body ("the Army") is able to respond to many different voices ("of the Voice"). The substance of the mental body ("the devas in their serried ranks") works ceaselessly, forming concrete thoughts as a response to sense impressions, emotional reactions, other concrete thoughts, wisdom, and insights ("work ceaselessly"). Through inquiry into your mental operations, apply yourself to discover the circumstances in which your mental body responds to each of the different types of voices ("let the disciple apply himself to the consideration of their methods"). In particular, investigate the stages of mental activity that must occur before wisdom and insights can be present. After you study, practice, and master these stages, your mind can inquire into the outer world of phenomena without being distorted by the illusions of the mental plane ("let him learn the rules whereby that Army works within the veils of Maya").

The tenth rule essentially advises the study and practice of raja yoga, a system that requires controlling and disciplining the mind. According to this yoga, a person must pass through several mental stages before his or her perception can be illumined. The initial stages are concentration (the effort to remain focused on a particular seed thought) and meditation (the effort to think creatively regarding the seed thought while bringing through needed abstract ideas from the soul). These initial stages are described next; more advanced ones are considered in the eleventh rule.

Table 5 provides an outline of steps, originally published by Bailey, giving instruction on how to accomplish the concentration stage of raja yoga. The first three steps are preparatory. The first step is attaining physical comfort and control. Although the cross-legged position is often used in the East, the ordinary sitting position is probably easiest for a Westerner. In either case, the main requirements are to sit erect, with the spine in a straight line, and to sit relaxed, without slumping, so

Table 5. Meditation Outline—Steps to Develop Concentration

1.	The attainment of physical comfort and control.
2.	The breathing is noted as rhythmic and regular.
3.	Visualization of the threefold lower self (physical, emotional, and mental) as a. in contact with the soul. b. a channel for soul energy, through the medium of the mind, direct to the brain. From thence the physical mechanism can be controlled.
4.	Then a definite act of concentration, calling in the will. This involves an endeavor to keep the mind unmoving upon a certain form of words, so that their meaning is clear in our consciousness, and not the words themselves, or the fact that we are attempting to meditate.
5.	Then say, with focused attention: "More radiant than the sun, purer than the snow, subtler than the ether is the Self, the spirit within me. I am that Self. That Self am I."
6.	Concentrate now upon the words: "Thou God seest me." The mind is not permitted to falter in its concentration on their significance, meaning, and implications.
7.	Then, with deliberation bring the concentration work to a close, and say—again with the mind refocused on the underlying ideas—the following concluding statement: "There is a peace that passeth understanding; it abides in the hearts of those who live in the Eternal. There is a power that maketh all things new; it lives and moves in those who know the Self as one."

Source: A. A. Bailey, *From Intellect to Intuition* (1932; reprint; New York: Lucis Publishing Company, 1974), 228.

that there is no tenseness anywhere in the body.[12] The second step is paying close attention to your breathing. Here you may wish to use the pranayama exercise discussed in the fourth rule in chapter 2, or you may wish to do no more than ensure that your breathing is quiet and regular. The third step is the visualization exercise described in the ninth rule, which brings the personality into alignment with the soul.

The sixth step in Table 5 is concentration on a set of words that veils an abstract truth, and the suggested seed thought is "Thou God seest me." However, you may wish to replace it with some other verse or phrase, perhaps a passage from the Bible, or even one of the symbolic rules discussed in this book.

Because the objective of this step is to understand the truth that is veiled by the words, there should be no mechanical repetition of the words, such as in chanting. Through developing an intense interest in the seed thought, you can inhibit other mental activities from occurring without requiring any deliberate effort of suppression or control.

The outline in Table 5 is definitely a beginner's approach to meditation. If you have achieved the first initiation, you must have already mastered the concentration stage of raja yoga, as evidenced in your concentration on your meditation work or in your dedication to humanitarian efforts. Before achieving the second initiation, you must also master the meditation stage. How can this next stage be accomplished? After concentrating on the seed thought, you may be able to sense the abstract truth veiled by the seed thought. If and when you do sense this truth, at that point the meditation stage begins. The next step is to bring the truth down to the mental body. At first you may have difficulty in grasping and touching the truth. But the struggle to comprehend leads to results, and little by little the idea seeps down to the concrete levels of the mental plane, where it can be appropriated as a basis for thought. Next, slowly build a thoughtform that embodies as much of the truth as can be brought through into your consciousness. While doing this building, you may have a desire to manifest your new understanding in some way on the physical plane. Thus, as a typical last step in the meditation stage, make plans to materialize, express, or communicate the truth to others.[13]

Rule Eleven

Let the disciple transfer the fire from the lower triangle to the higher, and preserve that which is created through the fire of the midway point.[14]

According to the eighth through tenth rules, several methods of meditation are recommended during the period between the first and second initiations: receptive meditation, building the first half of the antahkarana, inquiry into the operations of the mind, and the first two stages of raja yoga. The remaining rules give instruction for the period between the second and third initiations. To understand those rules, it is helpful to consider the nature of the soul in more detail.

As indicated in Table 4, each etheric chakra can be symbolized as a lotus consisting of a specific number of petals. The soul is constructed with matter from the abstract levels of the mental plane, and it also can be symbolized as a lotus, sometimes called the "egoic lotus." This lotus has nine outer petals that radiate from a common center and hide within themselves three central petals, so that there are twelve petals altogether. The three central petals represent the point where a threefold energy from the spiritual triad is anchored in the egoic lotus, and the nine outer petals are created by the response of the mental plane to that energy. The vibratory capacity of these petals represents the consciousness aspect of a human being: the opportunity to express abstract thought, the innate potential to progress, and the ability to function as a self-conscious entity.[15]

Each outer petal has a particular meaning. These outer petals are arranged in three concentric circles, with three petals in each circle. The petals in the largest circle are called the *knowledge* petals. They represent the wisdom, or abstracted essence of knowledge, that enables a person to demonstrate intelligent activity on the physical plane. The petals in the middle circle are called the *love* petals and represent the application of wisdom for transforming self-centered feelings into inclusive love. The petals in the inner circle are called the *sacrifice* petals, referring to the sacrifice of materialistic goals. They represent the application of love and wisdom for the purpose of serving humanity. Thus, the knowledge, love, and sacrifice petals symbolize the three aspects of the soul discussed in chapter 1: wisdom, inclusive love, and will or purpose.[16]

The symbology of the egoic lotus provides an image of how the different qualities of the soul unfold over time. For an undeveloped person, the egoic lotus is described as having the appearance of an unopened bud; but during the course of evolution, the petals slowly become organized, vitalized, and then opened. When a person starts on the path of probation, the largest circle of petals has already opened. When the first initiation is taken, the middle circle of petals has opened. When the second initiation is reached, the forces embodied in the two outer circles of petals are coordinated and interactive. By the time the third initiation is attained, the third circle of petals must also be unfolded.[17] There is a close interrelationship among the following factors: the unfolding of the petals of the egoic lotus; the awakening of the seven head centers, mentioned in the eighth rule; the awakening of the seven major etheric chakras; the dissipation of the etheric webs discussed in chapter 2; the movement of energies in the etheric body; and the activity of the endocrine glands.

In the eleventh rule, the symbols have the following interpretations: "the fire" refers to consciousness; "lower triangle," to the personality, consisting of the mental, emotional, and physical bodies; "higher" triangle, to the soul, consisting of the will, love, and wisdom aspects; and "midway point," to the illumined mind.

When disciples have reached the stage of development represented by the eleventh rule, they have taken the second initiation and are able to deepen their practice of meditation by achieving the advanced stages of raja yoga. This deeper method involves applying the mind to some problem for helping the human race. The first step is the alignment exercise described in the ninth rule. The second step is proceeding through the stages learned in the tenth rule, which means concentrating and meditating on the chosen problem.

The third step is the contemplation stage of raja yoga, and it is described in the first phrase of the eleventh rule. To achieve this step, you should temporarily shift the polarization of consciousness from the personality to the soul ("let the disciple transfer the fire from the lower triangle to the higher"). In particular, merge the self-will of the personality with the will aspect of the soul, replace selfish feelings with the love aspect of the soul, and negate the activity of the concrete mind while expressing the wisdom aspect of the soul. Through this process, learn to function as the soul in its own world, contemplating the world of meaning that lies behind the particular problem being studied. Meanwhile, the concrete mind is quiescent and oriented toward receiving abstract ideas from the soul. Prior to the third initiation, the contemplation stage can be held for only a brief period. It ends when the polarization of consciousness slips back into the personality.[18]

The fourth step is the illumination stage of raja yoga; it is described in the second phrase of the eleventh rule. Because the ideas created by the soul are abstract in nature, they tend to be nebulous and fleeting. Thus, you should preserve those ideas through the activity of the illumined mind ("and preserve that which is created through the fire of the midway point"). In particular, convert those ideas into understanding through the following efforts: appropriating knowledge as the foundation for wisdom, adapting the things of form to the life of the spirit, and relating the facts of the material world to universal principles.[19]

By comparing the character-building and meditation interpretations for the first phrase of the eleventh rule, it can be seen that they are essentially the same: They aim at achieving the same stage of contemplation but with a different emphasis. Whereas the character-building version has to do with transferring the energies of the lower chakras into the higher ones, the meditation version deals with transferring the polarization of consciousness into the soul. The two processes of character building and meditation overlap at this rule because achieving the contemplation stage is an essential prerequisite for accomplishing the remaining rules in both processes.

Rule Twelve

Let the disciple learn the use of the hand in service;
let him seek the mark of the messenger in his feet,
and let him learn to see with the eye that looks out
from between the two.[20]

The various stages of raja yoga were described in the two
preceding sections and can be interpreted in terms of shifting
the polarization of consciousness. In the concentration stage,
consciousness is drawn away from the physical body and
becomes polarized in the emotional body. In the meditation
stage, consciousness is drawn away from the emotional body
and becomes polarized in the realm of concrete thought, or the
mental body. In the contemplation stage, consciousness is
shifted even higher and becomes polarized in the realm of
abstract thought, or the soul. In the illumination stage, the
polarization shifts back into the mental body, allowing abstract
ideas to be transformed into understanding. Each of these
stages leads sequentially to the next. By mastering these stages,
disciples can unfold the three major powers of the illumined
mind: the power of healing, the power of intuitional response,
and the power of spiritual perception. Each of these powers is
described by a phrase in the twelfth rule.

The first phrase in this rule is "let the disciple learn the use
of the hand in service." In addition to the seven major chakras,
there are also twenty-one minor energy centers in the etheric
body. According to this phrase, you should learn to utilize the
minor chakra in each hand for the purpose of blessing, sometimes called radiatory healing. The first step is experiencing
inner peace, compassion, and mental clarity, which can be
done by achieving the illumination stage of raja yoga. The next
step is using the hands to transmit those same qualities to
various recipients, thereby helping them to calm their emotions, experience compassion, and strengthen their minds.[21]

The second phrase is "let him seek the mark of the messenger in his feet." Hermes was known as the Messenger of the

Gods in Greek mythology, corresponding to Mercury in Roman mythology. He was usually pictured as wearing winged sandals, and this phrase refers to those sandals. As the divine intermediary, Hermes carried messages from Zeus, who was both his father and the supreme ruler of the gods, to human beings. Because the intuitional power acts as the intermediary between the spiritual and human dimensions of life, Hermes symbolizes that power. Thus, this phrase means that you should work on awakening your intuitional power. The necessary approach is to establish a point of invocative tension in the lower pole of a given polarity and then receive the intuition generated by the evocative response of the higher pole. Through this process, you can bring into increasing rapport three different polarities: your lower concrete mind and spiritual mind, enabling you to receive insights; yourself and a Master of the Wisdom, enabling you to receive inspiration regarding your service activities; and yourself and the spiritual kingdom of nature as a whole, enabling you to receive a synthetic realization of the divine plan.[22]

The first two polarities were discussed as part of the third and seventh rules for meditation. During the early stages of the path of discipleship, it is possible to receive only brief glimpses of insight and inspiration because the conditions necessary for a more frequent occurrence are not yet present. But by reaching the stage represented by the second phrase of the twelfth rule, you have provided the right conditions: development of the faculty of abstract thought during the contemplation stage of raja yoga, dispelling of mental illusions during the illumination stage, and cultivation of the ability to serve, such as in the form of radiatory healing.

Let us consider the third polarity in more detail. While you are bringing the first two polarities into increasing rapport, the will aspect of your soul steadily becomes more dominant. As a result, the emphasis of your life slowly shifts from individual self-betterment, which is initially selfish but tends eventually toward selflessness, to service as part of a group, which involves the stages of group unity, group meditation, and group activity, and then to service that links and blends the work of various groups. When you reach that final step, your consciousness is no longer confined to any one group, and you are able to bring yourself into increasing rapport with the spiritual kingdom of nature as a whole. Thus, you are able to awaken your intuitional power even further and increasingly comprehend the unity of the divine plan as it is being expressed through all groups listed in Table 2. This awakening leads to more cooperation with others and more impersonality in your service.[23]

The third phrase is "let him learn to see with the eye that looks out from between the two." A human being consists of personality, soul, and spirit, and the soul can be thought of as being an eye that looks out between the personality and the spirit. This phrase refers to the power of spiritual perception, which uses the light of the soul to recognize the divinity lying behind all phenomenal appearances. To unfold this power, you must first develop and stabilize the ability to achieve fusion with your soul, which is the contemplation stage. Next, use the light of your soul to perceive the vision of the soul lying behind every physical form. Finally, use that light to reveal the spirit aspect lying even further behind, which is the Presence of Deity and is both immanent and transcendent.[24]

To carry out that final step and recognize the Presence of Deity, you must work toward an increasing release from emotional and mental ties of any kind, though not a release from physical conditions and responsibilities. What is required is an inner attitude of complete abandonment to the will of the soul. Cultivate simplicity of thought, remembering that an undue concern regarding people and conditions indicates mental activity but not soul understanding. Strive for soul activity, and then learn to perceive that which absorbs all dualities and causes all distinctions and differences to lose their meaning. Through this process, you can be dimly and faintly sensitive to the great Whole that lies behind the subjective world of souls, just as that subjective world lies behind the physical, tangible world of everyday life.[25]

Rule Thirteen

Four things the disciple must learn and comprehend before he can be shewn that inmost mystery: first, the laws of that which radiates; the five meanings of magnetization make the second; the third is transmutation, or the secret lost of alchemy; and lastly the first letter of the Word which has been imparted, or the hidden name egoic.[26]

By awakening their intuitional power, disciples are able to apprehend the ideas and significances embodying the immediate aspect of the divine plan for humanity. They also gain an intuitive understanding of the part they may play in that evolutionary process. At the stage of the spiritual path represented by the thirteenth rule, their part includes using telepathic communication to help disseminate the new ideas. This work involves finding individuals who might be responsive and then impressing their minds with the ideas. Those individuals can then carry the new concepts deeper into the mass of humanity.

Because of distrust about their intention, point of view, and motives, disciples have many questions about this type of work: Does anyone have the right to work telepathically on the mind of another person? How do subtle interactions occur, and are there any safeguards? And how can a recipient be impressed and still be left free? Disciples realize that telepathic interactions occur all the time, generally unconsciously and without skill or purpose, but they also realize that they must thoroughly prepare themselves before undertaking the work of deliberately impressing the minds of others.

There are four facets of telepathic communication that disciples must learn and comprehend ("four things the disciple must learn and comprehend") before they can produce outer results that are intelligently and harmoniously in line with the inner divine plan ("before he can be shewn that inmost mystery"). Each of these facets is described by a phrase in the thirteenth rule.

First, disciples must learn "the laws of that which radiates." Because telepathy is based on the outgoing vibratory effect of the etheric chakras, disciples must know the laws of the chakras. Five different types of telepathic impressions can be sent or received with the chakras. Abstract thoughts, referring to a nonverbal understanding of ideas, can be sent by the transmitter's crown and brow chakras and be registered by the recipient's crown chakra. Concrete thoughts can be sent by the throat and solar plexus chakras and be registered by the same chakras in the recipient. Higher emotions, such as compassion and devotion, can be sent and registered by the heart chakra. Lower emotions, such as fear and desire, can be sent and registered by the solar plexus chakra. Sensual impulses, concerning physical comfort and appetites, can be sent by the splenic chakra and be registered by the sacral chakra. However, the capacity to transmit or register a particular type of impression depends on the activity in the associated chakras. During the period between the second and third initiations, disciples have the capacity to transmit all of the above impressions except abstract thoughts. They can transmit abstract thoughts only after attaining the third initiation.[27]

Although the words *intuitional*, *telepathic*, and *psychic* all refer to sensing subtle energies, meaningful distinctions can be made between them. As described in the preceding section, intuitional sensitivity can apprehend insights, inspiration, and the divine plan. This sensitivity uses the abstract levels of the mental plane as its medium of communication and is based on the unfoldment of the egoic lotus. Telepathic sensitivity uses the planetary etheric body as its medium of communication and is based on activity in the etheric chakras. The etheric body of every form in nature is an integral part of the planetary etheric body, which in turn is part of the physical plane. Psychic sensitivity uses the astral plane as its medium of communication and is based on two factors: activity in the astral counterparts of the etheric chakras and an opening in the etheric web that separates the etheric and astral chakras, enabling psychic impressions to pass into the etheric body and be registered in the physical brain. At the stage on the spiritual path represented by the thirteenth rule, disciples have the capacity to be both intuitive and telepathic, but they may not be psychic. Because of the fundamental differences between these modes of communication, telepathic work can be carried forward without requiring any psychic unfoldment in either the transmitter or the receiver.

Second, disciples must know "the five meanings of magnetization." The fourth rule in chapter 2 referred to prana, which is the Sanskrit name for the energy of vitality in the etheric body. In the year 1774, Franz Anton Mesmer discovered this energy and named it "animal magnetism."[28] Bailey herself sometimes calls this energy animal magnetism or, simply, magnetism.[29] Prana is absorbed from the atmosphere by the splenic chakra. Afterward, according to yoga philosophy, the absorbed prana is differentiated into five specialized types that are then distributed throughout the etheric body. Thus, the "five meanings of magnetization" refers to the five specialized types of prana. Table 6 on page 90 lists the Sanskrit names for these five types, the traditional definitions from yoga, and the definitions given by Bailey. Telepathic communication is closely related to the movement of prana. To transmit any type of telepathic impression, one must know how to record the impression on the appropriate specialized type of prana and then direct the movement of that blended energy to the recipient.[30]

Third, disciples must understand "transmutation, or the secret lost of alchemy." In any form of telepathic work, feelings of positive regard and love constitute the coherent quality that links together the transmitter and the recipient. Thus, to establish a telepathic rapport, disciples must transmute any critical

Table 6. The Five Differentiations of Prana

Type	Traditional Definition	Bailey Definition
Prana	"It controls our breathing, and enables us to draw in the universal Life-forces into our physical being."	"Prana, extending from the nose to the heart and having special relation to the mouth and speech, the heart and lungs."
Vyana	"The life-breath which governs the circulations in the body, and hence is that which . . . keeps the body in shape."	"Its instruments are the thousands of nadis or nerves found in the body, and it has a peculiar definite connection with the blood channels, and veins and arteries."
Samana	"The life-breath which controls digestion and assimilation, and hence is that which carries on the chemical processes."	"Samana extends from the heart to the solar plexus; it concerns food and the nourishing of the body."
Apana	"The life-breath which casts out of the human system all that is waste material, the death force of the lower part of the body."	"Apana controls from the solar plexus to the soles of the feet; it concerns the organs of elimination, of rejection and of birth."
Upana	"The life-breath which directs the vital currents of the body upward to their sources, to the higher centers of their being."	"Upana is found between the nose and the top of the head; it has a special relation to the brain, the nose and the eyes."

Sources: J. M. Tyberg, *Language of the Gods* (Los Angeles: East-West Cultural Centre, 1970), 102–103; A. A. Bailey, *The Light of the Soul* (1927; reprint; New York: Lucis Publishing Company, 1978), 329–330.

feelings they might have regarding those whom they are seeking to help and strengthen. The lost secret of alchemy is how base metals can be transmuted into gold through the agency of fire and how this transmutation can occur by affecting the greater, or controlling, devas, rather than working directly on the lesser devas that form the substance of the metals.[31] In the case of telepathic work, disciples must know how critical feelings can be transmuted into positive regard and love through the agency of the illumined mind and how this transmutation can occur by affecting the underlying thoughts and beliefs, rather than working directly on the actual feelings. The following are some specific and brief precepts to aid in carrying out this transmutation. Observe the contents of the mind, and work consciously at purifying the mind of all prejudice, preconceived ideas, and hasty judgments. Practice harmlessness in thought and word. Refuse to think unkindly or with criticism regarding those whose minds are to be impressed. And maintain complete and unbroken silence concerning the telepathic work.[32]

Before interpreting the fourth phrase, it is necessary to give some additional definitions. Just as a human being consists of a personality, a soul, and a spirit, the planetary life can also be thought of as having those divisions. The fourth, or human, kingdom is the planetary personality; and the fifth, or spiritual, kingdom is the planetary soul. In theosophy, the name of the planetary spirit (or Logos) is said to be *Sanat Kumara*, which is a Sanskrit expression meaning "the eternal divine youth." However, that name is symbolic. The hidden nature, or "name," of the planetary spirit is divine will or purpose. It consists of seven different types, or "letters," listed in Table 7 on page 92. Individuals can experience these various types but only in a progressive way. Before reaching the fourth initiation, they can experience no more than the initial phase of divine will, which is the will to express the divine plan. This phase is the seventh type listed in Table 7 and is symbolized in Hinduism with the word *O.M.* After the fourth initiation, individuals can begin to sense the sixth type listed in Table 7.[33]

On the path of discipleship, the primary efforts are to unfold the love nature, achieve illumination, allow the intuitional power of the soul to function and be in control, and respond to the planetary soul (or spiritual kingdom of nature). The path of discipleship ends with the third initiation, at which point the path of initiation begins. On the path of initiation, the primary efforts are to unfold the will nature (as outlined in Table 7), achieve synthesis, allow the dynamic purpose of the

Table 7. The Seven Types of Divine Will

Type	Name	Description
One	The will to initiate	"The unknown, unseen and unheard purpose of Sanat Kumara. It is the secret of life itself and is known only to Him alone."
Two	The will to unify	"The purpose underlying revelation"
Three	The will to evolve	"The (as yet) unrecognized purpose which evoked the creative activity of our Planetary Logos"
Four	The will to harmonize or relate	"The mysterious purpose which has necessitated the calling into activity the Principle of Pain"
Five	The will to act	"[This] purpose of Sanat Kumara is related in a peculiar sense to the cyclic manifestation of all that is found in the three worlds of human evolution."
Six	The will to cause	The purpose that underlies or causes the divine plan
Seven	The will to express	The purpose of expressing or cooperating with the divine plan

Sources: A. A. Bailey, *The Rays and the Initiations* (1960; reprint; New York: Lucis Publishing Company, 1976), 241–247; A. A. Bailey, *Esoteric Astrology* (1951; reprint; New York: Lucis Publishing Company, 1979), 605.

spirit to function and be in control, and respond to the planetary spirit (or Logos). The seventh rule in chapter 1 anticipated some of the practices belonging to the path of discipleship and incorporated them into the final portion of the path of probation. Similarly, the fourth phrase of the thirteenth rule anticipates some of the practices belonging to the path of initiation and incorporates them into the final portion of the path of discipleship.[34]

Let us now consider the fourth phrase. Disciples must learn and comprehend "the first letter of the Word which has been imparted." This injunction has the following meaning: Before beginning their telepathic work, disciples must invoke the initial phase of the will energy that has been imparted from the planetary spirit. When evoked, this phase dimly reveals the hidden nature of the exalted divine consciousness that has brought our planet and all that is within and upon it into being ("the hidden name egoic"). In particular, this phase is an immanent, propulsive, clarifying, stabilizing, and driving force, demonstrating as an absorbing devotion to the divine plan and an effort to serve that plan, at any cost, as it is progressively understood and grasped.[35]

To clarify these concepts, it may be helpful to contrast three different types of will. The will of the personality, or desire, applies emotional energy and knowledge for the purpose of achieving self-centered ambition. The will of the soul is sometimes called *goodwill*, and it applies love and wisdom for the purpose of serving humanity. The initial phase of divine will is sometimes called the *will-to-good*, and it applies spiritual perception and intuition for the purpose of serving the divine plan.

What is the difference between service motivated by goodwill and service motivated by the will-to-good? People of goodwill are idealistic and work to manifest some vision of a better world, but that vision may be limited and incomplete. For instance, they might work to make material life easier for others or to promote national or international peace. However, there is a goal greater than easy material conditions or world peace, and that goal is the good of the whole. People motivated by the will-to-good can think in terms of the whole, understand the lessons of the past, and appreciate the next step to be taken for improving the welfare of the whole. That next step is the immediate aspect of the divine plan, but it may not make material life easier or bring about peaceful conditions. Instead, the divine plan involves establishing those arrangements and circumstances that can expand the consciousness of humankind, enabling human beings to discover the spiritual values *for themselves* and to make the needed changes *of their own free will*.[36]

After evoking the will-to-good, disciples can proceed with their telepathic work because they are motivated to serve the divine plan in three important respects. First, they carry the work forward selflessly, with freedom from personal prejudice and personal choices. Second, by applying the power of spiritual perception, they appreciate and respect the inner divinity of any recipient, including the latter's right to make choices based on his or her own free will. Thus, they only offer new ideas for consideration, rather than imposing some direction or form of pressure. Third, by means of their intuitive contact with the divine plan, they offer ideas that outline or are based on that plan, such as the concept that separation is a thing of the past, and unity is the goal of the immediate future; or that hatred is undesirable, and goodwill will transform the world.[37]

Rule Fourteen

Listen, touch, see, apply, know.[38]

When nearing the end of the path of discipleship, disciples are primarily occupied with world affairs. They understand that the outer happenings in the world are predictable to some extent because those happenings are the precipitated effects of hidden causes that lie deep within the subconsciousness of humanity. They also understand that those causes can be noted and then offset or stimulated to a certain point. Consequently, they are ready to learn and apply a systematic technique for working in the world of causes, whereas most people are still involved in the world of effects. This technique, described in the fourteenth rule, is based on combining the three spiritual powers discussed in the twelfth rule with the four facets of telepathy discussed in the thirteenth rule.[39]

The fourteenth rule consists of five words, and the first word is "listen." The sound that should be listened to is the will-to-good, which is the will to express or cooperate with the divine plan. This listening involves merging the personality self-will with the sacrificial will of the soul and then invoking the divine will. In the alignment process described in the ninth rule, the first half of the antahkarana is built, which is equivalent to merging the personality with the soul. Here, however, the entire antahkarana is constructed, which merges the personality, soul, and spiritual triad.

The second word is "touch." After evoking the divine will, the next step is to use the intuitional power to touch the divine plan. This touching involves negating the activity of the lower, or concrete, mind and then subordinating the wisdom aspect of the soul to the higher lights of insight, inspiration, and synthetic realization. Through these efforts, it is possible to contact, touch, and then grasp the new ideas that are associated with the next step to be taken in world evolution.

The third word is "see," which refers to releasing the power of spiritual perception. This also involves two efforts. The first is to apply the alchemical precepts mentioned in the thirteenth rule to transmute any feelings of judgment or criticism for the individuals who are to be helped and strengthened. By transmuting those feelings into positive regard and love, it is possible to establish a telepathic rapport with the recipients. The second effort is to perceive those individuals in a spiritual sense, recognizing their inner divinity and their right to remain free of any mental or emotional pressure. After these preliminary efforts have been made, the telepathic work can begin.

The fourth word is "apply." The twelfth rule described the power of healing, and the thirteenth rule described certain laws regarding the radiation of energy from chakras and the movement of prana. Through application of that power and those laws of telepathy, thoughtforms can be projected that offer the new ideas plus the qualities of inner peace, compassion, and mental clarity. In this way, the new ideas can be transmitted to various political, economic, or religious leaders who may not be sufficiently intuitive to receive the ideas directly for themselves. In addition, those leaders can be protected with a guarding wall of light and love, enabling them to withstand the tide of destructive criticism that material-minded people continually pour out upon them.[40]

The fifth word is "know." At present, many conflicting teachings regarding meditation are being promoted. In this circumstance, the Bible counsels us to test those teachings by examining the results obtained from following them: "Wherefore by their fruits ye shall know them" (Matt. 7:20). The fruitage of a successful meditation practice is realized knowledge. Following the rules for meditation presented in this chapter will bring several kinds of knowledge: firsthand experience with the different stages of raja yoga, awareness of the relationship between the human kingdom of nature and the spiritual kingdom, appreciation of the immediate aspect of the divine plan, practical skills in healing and telepathic work, and progressive mastery over the personality, culminating in the knowledge and experience of the third initiation.

Chapter 5

The Seven Rays

This book has reviewed Bailey's fourteen rules for spiritual initiation. Each of the preceding chapters has examined seven of those rules and shown that they constitute a sevenfold process of training for either the path of probation or the path of discipleship and for either character building or meditation. We will consider next the relationship between these rules and the typology of the seven rays.

In the commentary for the thirteenth rule in chapter 3, the typology of the seven rays was introduced. The ray of an energy refers to the quality rather than the appearance of the energy, implying that the same ray can be expressed by various energies having different form aspects. Table 3 in chapter 3 lists the name and basic quality for each ray. Since each of the seven rays can be further divided into seven subrays, this typology defines a hierarchical system: The top level represents a particular energy, the second level consists of the seven rays, or qualities, of that energy, and the third level consists of the subrays of each ray.

As an example, suppose that the top level represents soul energy. Because the soul of each human being is expressive of

one particular ray, called the soul ray, the second level represents the seven types of soul rays. And because each soul ray
consists of seven different qualities of energy, the third level
represents those subrays.

Bailey's rules for initiation are related to the seven rays in
three different ways. First, these rules describe the intuitive
guidance received by an individual whose soul ray is specifi-
cally the second ray of love-wisdom. In general, the guidance
people receive from their souls depends on their soul rays.
However, the second ray is also the ray of the solar system,
implying that all other rays are subrays of the second ray.
Thus, the second-ray method of working on the spiritual path
forms the basis for all other techniques, and the differences
appear in what is emphasized.[1] Each ray's method of working
can be shown to be similar to an organized system of thought,
such as a traditional system of yoga. For instance, the method
for the second ray is similar to jnana yoga, which is the path of
wisdom. The methods of working for all seven rays are
described in detail and compared elsewhere.[2]

Second, the typology of the seven rays is involved in the
particular symbols used in the thirteenth rule. In the character-
building interpretation for that rule, the soul energy is divided
into seven different qualities of energy, corresponding to the
seven subrays of the soul ray. In the meditation interpretation,
the divine will is divided into seven different types. Because the
divine will represents first-ray energy, the seven types of divine
will correspond to the seven subrays of the first ray.

Third, each sevenfold process of training has the structure
of the seven rays. In other words, each rule within each process
carries the specific quality associated with the corresponding
ray. For either character building or meditation, each rule on
the path of probation is a lower form of the corresponding rule
on the path of discipleship, thereby revealing the spiral nature
of the spiritual path. These relationships are demonstrated by
the summaries that follow.

The first ray is that of will or power, and it has the quality of dynamic purpose. The first rule in each sevenfold process can be seen as characterizing the initiating purpose for the entire process. In chapter 1, that purpose is expressing inclusive love through outer behavior. In chapter 2, the purpose is raising the vibration of consciousness until it reaches that of the soul. In chapter 3, it is contacting the energies of the soul and then directing those energies through the mental, emotional, and etheric bodies. In chapter 4, it is shifting the polarization of consciousness into the soul.

The second ray is that of love-wisdom, and it has the quality of love. The second rule in each process establishes the context, or environment, that holds and supports the rest of the process. In chapter 1, that context is maintaining the cyclic rhythm of individual application. In chapter 2, the context is centering the consciousness as high as possible in the head. In chapter 3, it is being involved in the rhythm of group application. In chapter 4, it is building the first half of the antahkarana.

The third ray is that of active intelligence, and it has the quality of intellect. The third rule in each process describes how the intellect should be employed. In chapter 1, the intellect is used for purifying the personality through the invocation and evocation of higher energies. In chapter 2, the intellect is used for discovering underlying motives. In chapter 3, it is used for purifying emotional reactions through understanding the cause and meaning of those reactions. In chapter 4, the intellect itself is investigated to discover how it can receive illumination from the soul.

The seven rays are divided into two different groups: The first three rays are sometimes called the major rays or the rays of aspect, and the last four rays are sometimes called the minor rays or the rays of attribute.[3] Similarly, each sevenfold process of rules is also divided into two groups. In chapters 1 and 2, the first three rules correspond to the stage of Little Chelaship on the path of probation, and the last four rules correspond to the stage of Chela in the Light on that path. In chapters 3 and 4, the first three rules correspond to the period between the first and second initiations on the path of discipleship, and the last four rules correspond to the period between the second and third initiations on that path.

The fourth ray is that of harmony through conflict, and its quality is unification. The fourth rule in each process describes how different parts of a human being can be unified through the transfer of energy. In chapter 1, this rule describes the transfer of energy from the sacral chakra to the throat chakra and from the solar plexus chakra to the heart chakra. In chapter 2, the rule describes the practice of pranayama, which uses the transfer of prana to unify the dense physical and etheric bodies. In chapter 3, it describes both the upward and downward trends of energy in the etheric body. In chapter 4, it describes the transfer of polarization into the soul, which unifies the personality and soul.

The fifth ray is that of concrete knowledge or science, and its quality is discrimination. The fifth rule in each process differentiates between different members of the same category. In chapter 1, this rule differentiates between virtuous and non-virtuous behavior. In chapter 2, the rule differentiates between the voice of the soul and that of the personality. In chapter 3, it differentiates between three types of soul-infused behavior. In chapter 4, it differentiates between three powers of the illumined mind.

The sixth ray is that of devotion or idealism, and its quality is devoted sensitivity to an ideal. The sixth rule in each process indicates the ideal for that process and how devotion to the ideal is expressed. In chapter 1, the ideal displays inclusive love, and it is expressed by becoming a vegetarian. In chapter 2, the ideal works to manifest the plan of the soul and is expressed by making the needed corrections in the personality. In chapter 3, it displays the methods and techniques of the spiritual kingdom of nature and is expressed by learning four aspects of service. In chapter 4, it works to manifest the divine plan for humanity and is expressed by learning four facets of telepathic communication.

The seventh ray is that of ceremonial order, or magic, and it has the quality of producing the outer appearance of an inner reality. The seventh rule is the last in each sevenfold process, and it indicates the tangible fruitage of applying the rules for that process. In chapter 1, the fruitage is physical behavior guided by wisdom. In chapter 2, the fruitage is inspiration received during meditation. In chapter 3, it is service in both the physical and astral worlds that is guided by intuitive understanding. In chapter 4, it is realized knowledge concerning the subtle dimensions of life.

Bailey predicted the founding of a chain of publicly recognized schools to train students for spiritual initiation. These schools would be located in a number of countries, generally in areas that had training centers for the esoteric mysteries in the ancient past, and they would be administered by disciples who have been appointed by and receive inspiration from the Masters of the Wisdom.[4] Also according to Bailey, in the fourteen rules considered here you have one of the "great foundational courses" of the coming schools for initiation.[5]

Notes

Introduction

1. In A. A. Bailey, *Initiation, Human and Solar* (1922; reprint; New York: Lucis Publishing Company, 1974), 192, the fourteen symbolic rules are said to be "a series of instructions compiled for those who seek to take the first initiation." However, there is ambiguity in this statement because Bailey uses two different approaches for counting initiations. She emphasizes in many of her books that the third initiation from the human angle is regarded as only the first initiation from the standpoint of the spiritual kingdom of nature, and she sometimes shifts from one counting approach to the other. For instance, see A. A. Bailey, *Discipleship in the New Age*, vol. 1 (1944; reprint; New York: Lucis Publishing Company, 1976), 728. In this book, we will count initiations from only the human angle and will consider the symbolic rules as providing sequential instructions for both the paths of probation and discipleship, leading to the third initiation.

Chapter 1: Elementary Rules for Character Building

1. A. A. Bailey, *The Rays and the Initiations* (1960; reprint; New York: Lucis Publishing Company, 1976), 323.
2. A. A. Bailey, *Initiation, Human and Solar* (1922; reprint; New York: Lucis Publishing Company, 1974), 192.
3. A. A. Bailey, *Esoteric Psychology*, vol. 2 (1942; reprint; New York: Lucis Publishing Company, 1975), 427–428.
4. Bailey, *Initiation, Human and Solar*, 193.
5. A. A. Bailey, *Discipleship in the New Age*, vol. 1 (1944; reprint; New York: Lucis Publishing Company, 1976), 715–716.
6. A. A. Bailey, *A Treatise on White Magic* (1934; reprint; New York: Lucis Publishing Company, 1974), 323, 512–514.
7. Bailey, *Initiation, Human and Solar*, 194.
8. A. A. Bailey, *The Reappearance of the Christ* (1948; reprint; New York: Lucis Publishing Company, 1979), 157.
9. Bailey, *The Reappearance of the Christ*, 151; Bailey, *The Rays and the Initiations*, 35, 528.
10. A. A. Bailey, *Glamour: A World Problem* (1950; reprint; New York: Lucis Publishing Company, 1971), 247–264.
11. A. A. Bailey, *Esoteric Healing* (1953; reprint; New York: Lucis Publishing Company, 1977), 239–240; Bailey, *A Treatise on White Magic*, 197, 202–203.
12. Bailey, *A Treatise on White Magic*, 490–491; Bailey, *Discipleship in the New Age*, vol. 1, 474.
13. Bailey, *Initiation, Human and Solar*, 195.
14. Bailey, *Glamour: A World Problem*, 150.
15. Bailey, *The Rays and the Initiations*, 92.
16. Bailey, *Esoteric Psychology*, vol. 2, 524–525.
17. Bailey, *The Rays and the Initiations*, 669–671.
18. Bailey, *A Treatise on White Magic*, 504.
19. Bailey, *Esoteric Psychology*, vol. 2, 132.

20. Bailey, *Initiation, Human and Solar*, 195.

21. Bailey, *Discipleship in the New Age*, vol. 1, 719–722, 735–736.

22. A. A. Bailey, *Esoteric Psychology*, vol. 1 (1962; reprint; New York: Lucis Publishing Company, 1975), 284.

23. A. A. Bailey, *Letters on Occult Meditation* (1922; reprint; New York: Lucis Publishing Company, 1974), 146; Bailey, *Discipleship in the New Age*, vol. 1, 89–91.

24. Bailey, *Initiation, Human and Solar*, 196.

25. Bailey, *Esoteric Psychology*, vol. 1, 219–220.

26. Bailey, *Initiation, Human and Solar*, 196–198.

27. Bailey, *Initiation, Human and Solar*, 198.

28. A. A. Bailey, *Discipleship in the New Age*, vol. 2 (1955; reprint; New York: Lucis Publishing Company, 1972), 544–545, 554–556.

29. Bailey, *Discipleship in the New Age*, vol. 2, 557.

30. Bailey, *Discipleship in the New Age*, vol. 2, 556.

Chapter 2: Elementary Rules for Meditation

1. A. A. Bailey, *Initiation, Human and Solar* (1922; reprint; New York: Lucis Publishing Company, 1974), 192.

2. Z. F. Lansdowne, *The Chakras and Esoteric Healing* (York Beach, ME: Samuel Weiser, 1986), 34–39.

3. A. A. Bailey, *Esoteric Healing* (1953; reprint; New York: Lucis Publishing Company, 1977), 186–187, 202; A. A. Bailey, *A Treatise on White Magic* (1934; reprint; New York: Lucis Publishing Company, 1974), 591–592.

4. A. A. Bailey, *Letters on Occult Meditation* (1922; reprint; New York: Lucis Publishing Company, 1974), 95–96, 334–335.

5. Bailey, *A Treatise on White Magic*, 601–602.

6. Bailey, *A Treatise on White Magic*, 590.

7. Bailey, *Initiation, Human and Solar*, 193.

8. R. Assagioli, *Psychosynthesis* (1965; reprint; New York: Penguin Books, 1987), 22.

9. H. Chaudhuri, *Integral Yoga* (1965; reprint; San Francisco: California Institute of Asian Studies, 1970), 55-56.

10. Assagioli, *Psychosynthesis*, 111-120.

11. A. A. Bailey, *The Rays and the Initiations* (1960; reprint; New York: Lucis Publishing Company, 1976), 3.

12. Assagioli, *Psychosynthesis*, 119.

13. Bailey, *Initiation, Human and Solar*, 194.

14. Lansdowne, *The Chakras and Esoteric Healing*, 7-8.

15. Bailey, *The Rays and the Initiations*, 4-5.

16. Bailey, *Initiation, Human and Solar*, 199.

17. Bailey, *A Treatise on White Magic*, 201-203.

18. Bailey, *Initiation, Human and Solar*, 195.

19. Yogi Ramacharaka, *The Science of Psychic Healing* (1909; reprint; Chicago: Yogi Publication Society, 1937), 37.

20. E. Green and A. Green, *Beyond Biofeedback* (New York: Dell, 1977), 72-117.

21. A. A. Bailey, *The Light of the Soul* (1927; reprint; New York: Lucis Publishing Company, 1978), 219-220; Bailey, *A Treatise on White Magic*, 206-207.

22. A. A. Bailey, *Esoteric Psychology*, vol. 2 (1942; reprint; New York: Lucis Publishing Company, 1975), 595-596.

23. Bailey, *Initiation, Human and Solar*, 195.

24. A. A. Bailey, *Discipleship in the New Age*, vol. 2 (1955; reprint; New York: Lucis Publishing Company, 1972), 490.

25. A. A. Bailey, *Discipleship in the New Age*, vol. 1 (1944; reprint; New York: Lucis Publishing Company, 1976), 710-711.

26. Bailey, *A Treatise on White Magic*, 585.

27. A. A. Bailey, *The Destiny of the Nations* (1949; reprint; New York: Lucis Publishing Company, 1974), 44-45; Bailey, *A Treatise on White Magic*, 175.

28. Bailey, *Discipleship in the New Age*, vol. 2, 641-642.

29. Bailey, *Initiation, Human and Solar*, 196.

30. Bailey, *Discipleship in the New Age*, vol. 1, 708–709, 727.
31. A. A. Bailey, *Glamour: A World Problem* (1950; reprint; New York: Lucis Publishing Company, 1971), 256–257.
32. Bailey, *Initiation, Human and Solar*, 198.
33. Bailey, *The Rays and the Initiations*, 230.
34. Bailey, *A Treatise on White Magic*, 179–180.
35. Bailey, *Letters on Occult Meditation*, 266–269, 274.
36. Bailey, *A Treatise on White Magic*, 166, 179–180, 222.
37. Bailey, *Letters on Occult Meditation*, 276–277.

Chapter 3: Advanced Rules for Character Building

1. A. A. Bailey, *Initiation, Human and Solar* (1922; reprint; New York: Lucis Publishing Company, 1974), 200.
2. A. A. Bailey, *Esoteric Healing* (1953; reprint; New York: Lucis Publishing Company, 1977), 626.
3. A. A. Bailey, *The Rays and the Initiations* (1960; reprint; New York: Lucis Publishing Company, 1975), 155.
4. A. A. Bailey, *Glamour: A World Problem* (1950; reprint; New York: Lucis Publishing Company, 1971), 247–250; A. A. Bailey, *A Treatise on White Magic* (1934; reprint; New York: Lucis Publishing Company, 1974), 165–166.
5. Bailey, *Esoteric Healing*, 218, 625.
6. Bailey, *Esoteric Healing*, 613–614; Bailey, *The Rays and the Initiations*, 126–127.
7. Bailey, *Initiation, Human and Solar*, 202.
8. Bailey, *The Rays and the Initiations*, 152–153.
9. A. A. Bailey, *Discipleship in the New Age*, vol. 1 (1944; reprint; New York: Lucis Publishing Company, 1976), 144–145, 154–155.
10. Bailey, *Discipleship in the New Age*, vol. 1, 8–10.
11. Bailey, *The Rays and the Initiations*, 211–213.

12. A. A. Bailey, *Esoteric Psychology*, vol. 2 (1942; reprint; New York: Lucis Publishing Company, 1975), 193–194.

13. Bailey, *Initiation, Human and Solar*, 203.

14. A. A. Bailey, *A Treatise on Cosmic Fire* (1925; reprint; New York: Lucis Publishing Company, 1977), 667, 951–952; Bailey, *Initiation, Human and Solar*, 97.

15. Bailey, *Glamour: A World Problem*, 144–145.

16. Bailey, *Initiation, Human and Solar*, 204.

17. Bailey, *Esoteric Healing*, 214.

18. A. A. Bailey, *Education in the New Age* (1954; reprint; New York: Lucis Publishing Company, 1974), 62, 66, 82.

19. Bailey, *Esoteric Healing*, 215–216.

20. Bailey, *Initiation, Human and Solar*, 206.

21. Bailey, *Discipleship in the New Age*, vol. 1, 746.

22. Bailey, *Discipleship in the New Age*, vol. 1, 743–745.

23. A. A. Bailey, *Esoteric Psychology*, vol. 1 (1936; reprint; New York: Lucis Publishing Company, 1975), 290–291; A. A. Bailey, *Discipleship in the New Age*, vol. 2 (1955; reprint; New York: Lucis Publishing Company, 1972), 289–290.

24. Bailey, *A Treatise on Cosmic Fire*, 1010; Bailey, *A Treatise on White Magic*, 212–214.

25. Bailey, *Initiation, Human and Solar*, 207.

26. A. A. Bailey, *Esoteric Psychology*, vol. 1 (1936; reprint; New York: Lucis Publishing Company, 1975), 130; Bailey, *The Rays and the Initiations*, 157.

27. Bailey, *A Treatise on White Magic*, 125.

28. Bailey, *Esoteric Healing*, 214.

29. Bailey, *Esoteric Psychology*, vol. 1, 44.

30. A. A. Bailey, *The Externalisation of the Hierarchy* (1957; reprint; New York: Lucis Publishing Company, 1976), 29–30.

31. Bailey, *Esoteric Psychology*, vol. 2, 136–137.

32. Bailey, *Initiation, Human and Solar*, 208.

33. Bailey, *A Treatise on White Magic,* 175, 181, 304; A. A. Bailey, *Destiny of the Nations* (1949; reprint; New York: Lucis Publishing Company, 1974), 44-45.
34. Bailey, *Discipleship in the New Age*, vol. 1, 741-742.
35. Bailey, *Discipleship in the New Age*, vol. 1, 742.

Chapter 4: Advanced Rules for Meditation

1. A. A. Bailey, *Discipleship in the New Age*, vol. 2 (1955; reprint; New York: Lucis Publishing Company, 1972), 413-415; A. A. Bailey, *A Treatise on White Magic* (1934; reprint; New York: Lucis Publishing Company, 1974), 602.
2. A. A. Bailey, *Initiation, Human and Solar* (1922; reprint; New York: Lucis Publishing Company, 1974), 192.
3. C. W. Leadbeater, *The Chakras* (1927; reprint; Wheaton, IL: Theosophical Publishing House, 1977), 11-15; A. Avalon, *The Serpent Power* (1919; reprint; New York: Dover, 1974), 141.
4. A. A. Bailey, *A Treatise on Cosmic Fire* (1925; reprint; New York: Lucis Publishing Company, 1977), 183; Bailey, *Initiation, Human and Solar*, 200.
5. A. A. Bailey, *The Rays and the Initiations* (1960; reprint; New York: Lucis Publishing Company, 1975), 431-436.
6. Bailey, *A Treatise on White Magic*, 205-206; A. A. Bailey, *The Externalisation of the Hierarchy* (1957; reprint; New York: Lucis Publishing Company, 1976), 18-19.
7. Bailey, *Initiation, Human and Solar*, 202.
8. Bailey, *The Rays and the Initiations*, 467-469.
9. Bailey, *The Rays and the Initiations*, 487-488.
10. Bailey, *The Rays and the Initiations*, 488-490.
11. Bailey, *Initiation, Human and Solar*, 203.
12. A. A. Bailey, *From Intellect to Intuition* (1932; reprint; New York: Lucis Publishing Company, 1974), 218-220.
13. Bailey, *A Treatise on White Magic*, 366-368.

110   ZACHARY LANSDOWNE

14. Bailey, *Initiation, Human and Solar*, 204.
15. Bailey, *A Treatise on Cosmic Fire*, 710, 818.
16. Bailey, *A Treatise on Cosmic Fire*, 538–544, 767.
17. Bailey, *A Treatise on Cosmic Fire*, 543, 828, 830, 883.
18. Bailey, *From Intellect to Intuition*, 132–144.
19. Bailey, *From Intellect to Intuition*, 147–173; Bailey, *Initiation, Human and Solar*, 12.
20. Bailey, *Initiation, Human and Solar*, 206.
21. Z. F. Lansdowne, *The Chakras and Esoteric Healing* (York Beach, ME: Samuel Weiser, 1986), 79–87.
22. A. A. Bailey, *Esoteric Astrology* (1951; reprint; New York: Lucis Publishing Company, 1979), 353–354; Bailey, *The Rays and the Initiations*, 441.
23. Bailey, *The Rays and the Initiations*, 171, 173.
24. A. A. Bailey, *Glamour: A World Problem* (1950; reprint; New York: Lucis Publishing Company, 1971), 178–180.
25. A. A. Bailey, *Discipleship in the New Age*, vol. 1 (1944; reprint; New York: Lucis Publishing Company, 1976), 390–392.
26. Bailey, *Initiation, Human and Solar*, 207.
27. Lansdowne, *The Chakras and Esoteric Healing*, 66–77.
28. H. F. Ellenberger, *The Discovery of the Unconscious* (New York: Basic Books, 1970), 59.
29. Bailey, *Esoteric Healing*, 643–644.
30. A. A. Bailey, *Telepathy and the Etheric Vehicle* (1950; reprint; New York: Lucis Publishing Company, 1975), 27.
31. Bailey, *A Treatise on Cosmic Fire*, 476, 487.
32. Bailey, *Discipleship in the New Age*, vol. 1, 65–66.
33. Bailey, *The Rays and the Initiations*, 248, 263, 549.
34. Bailey, *Esoteric Astrology*, 613–614.
35. Bailey, *The Rays and the Initiations*, 49–50, 247.
36. Bailey, *Discipleship in the New Age*, vol. 2, 46–47, 270; Bailey, *The Externalisation of the Hierarchy*, 670.
37. Bailey, *Discipleship in the New Age*, vol. 1, 64–65.

38. Bailey, *Initiation, Human and Solar*, 208.
39. Bailey, *Discipleship in the New Age*, vol. 1, 705–706.
40. Bailey, *Discipleship in the New Age*, vol. 1, 705–706.

Chapter 5: The Seven Rays

1.   A. A. Bailey, *Discipleship in the New Age*, vol. 1 (1944; reprint; New York: Lucis Publishing Company, 1976), 711; A. A. Bailey, *Esoteric Psychology*, vol. 2 (1942; reprint; New York: Lucis Publishing Company, 1975), 110–111, 358.
2.   Z. F. Lansdowne, *The Rays and Esoteric Psychology* (York Beach, ME: Samuel Weiser, 1989).
3.   A. A. Bailey, *Esoteric Psychology*, vol. 1 (1936; reprint; New York: Lucis Publishing Company, 1975), 44, 421–422.
4.   A. A. Bailey, *Letters on Occult Meditation* (1922; reprint; New York: Lucis Publishing Company, 1974), 297–331.
5.   A. A. Bailey, *The Rays and the Initiations* (1960; reprint; New York: Lucis Publishing Company, 1976), 262.

Bibliography

Assagioli, R. *Psychosynthesis*. 1965. Reprint. New York: Penguin Books, 1987.

Avalon, A. *The Serpent Power*. 1919. Reprint. New York: Dover, 1974.

Bailey, A. A. *The Destiny of the Nations*. 1949. Reprint. New York: Lucis Publishing Company, 1974.

_____. *Discipleship in the New Age*, vol. 1. 1944. Reprint. New York: Lucis Publishing Company, 1976.

_____. *Discipleship in the New Age*, vol. 2. 1955. Reprint. New York: Lucis Publishing Company, 1972.

_____. *Education in the New Age*. 1954. Reprint. New York: Lucis Publishing Company, 1974.

_____. *Esoteric Astrology*. 1951. Reprint. New York: Lucis Publishing Company, 1979.

_____. *Esoteric Healing*. 1953. Reprint. New York: Lucis Publishing Company, 1977.

_____. *Esoteric Psychology*, vol. 1. 1936. Reprint. New York: Lucis Publishing Company, 1975.

_____. *Esoteric Psychology*, vol. 2. 1942. Reprint. New York: Lucis Publishing Company, 1975.

_____. *The Externalisation of the Hierarchy*. 1957. Reprint. New York: Lucis Publishing Company, 1976.

_____. *From Intellect to Intuition*. 1932. Reprint. New York: Lucis Publishing Company, 1974.

_____. *Glamour: A World Problem*. 1950. Reprint. New York: Lucis Publishing Company, 1971.

_____. *Initiation, Human and Solar*. 1922. Reprint. New York: Lucis Publishing Company, 1974.

_____. *Letters on Occult Meditation*. 1922. Reprint. New York: Lucis Publishing Company, 1974.

_____. *The Light of the Soul*. 1927. Reprint. New York: Lucis Publishing Company, 1978.

_____. *The Rays and the Initiations*. 1960. Reprint. New York: Lucis Publishing Company, 1976.

_____. *The Reappearance of the Christ*. 1948. Reprint. New York: Lucis Publishing Company, 1979.

_____. *The Soul and Its Mechanism*. 1930. Reprint. New York: Lucis Publishing Company, 1976.

_____. *Telepathy and the Etheric Vehicle*. 1950. Reprint. New York: Lucis Publishing Company, 1975.

_____. *A Treatise on Cosmic Fire*. 1925. Reprint. New York: Lucis Publishing Company, 1977.

_____. *A Treatise on White Magic*. 1934. Reprint. New York: Lucis Publishing Company, 1974.

Chaudhuri, H. *Integral Yoga*. 1965. Reprint. San Francisco: California Institute of Asian Studies, 1970.

Ellenberger, H. F. *The Discovery of the Unconscious*. New York: Basic Books, 1970.

Green, E., and A. Green. *Beyond Biofeedback*. New York: Dell, 1977.

Lansdowne, Z. F. *The Chakras and Esoteric Healing*. York Beach, ME: Samuel Weiser, Inc., 1986.

_____. *The Rays and Esoteric Psychology*. York Beach, ME: Samuel Weiser, Inc., 1989.

Leadbeater, C. W. *The Chakras*. 1927. Reprint. Wheaton, IL: Theosophical Publishing House, 1977.

Ramacharaka, Yogi. *The Science of Psychic Healing*. 1909. Reprint. Chicago: Yogi Publication Society, 1937.

Tyberg, J. M. *The Language of the Gods*. Los Angeles: East-West Cultural Centre, 1970.

About the Author

Zachary Lansdowne holds a Masters degree in engineering from the Massachusetts Institute of Technology, a Masters degree in philosophy and religion from the California Institute of Integral Studies, a Masters degree in clinical psychology from Antioch University and a Ph.D. in engineering from Stanford University. He is also the author of *The Chakras and Esoteric Healing* and *The Rays and Esoteric Psychology*, both published by Samuel Weiser.

He was a licensed spiritual healer and counselor with the Light Foundation in California for many years. He recently moved to Massachusetts where he is employed as a public policy analyst. He still maintains his interest in counseling and healing work.